Driving High

DRIVING HIGH

The Hazards of Driving, Drinking, and Drugs

by L.B. Taylor, Jr.

FRANKLIN WATTS
NEW YORK ■ LONDON ■ TORONTO
SYDNEY ■ 1983
A GROLIER COMPANY

FOR MICHAEL BILLINGS

Photographs courtesy of:
Wide World Photos: p. 7; and
United Press International: pp. 22, 27,
39, 45, 57, 75, 80, and 101.

Library of Congress Cataloging in Publication Data

Taylor, L. B.
Driving high:
The hazards of driving, drinking, and drugs.

Bibliography: p.
Includes index.
Summary: Describes the hazards of combining drinking
and drugs with driving and discusses ways both
in effect and under consideration for lessening the
grim statistics pertaining to this problem.
1. Drinking and traffic accidents—United States
—Juvenile literature.   2. Automobile drivers—
United States—Drug use—Juvenile literature.   [1.
Drinking and traffic accidents.   2. Automobile
drivers—Drug use.   3. Traffic accidents]   I. Title.
HE5620.D7T39 1983   363.1'251   83-6821
ISBN 0-531-04663-X

Contents

Driving
High

1
The Crash

It was 1:35 A.M., Saturday morning. Jeff, a seventeen-year-old high school junior, was behind the wheel of his father's car, a 1981 Oldsmobile Cutlass Supreme. He was on his way home after a night of partying. He had had too much to drink.

After some "cruising" earlier in the evening, he and four of his buddies had gone through a case of beer. Then later, as his "buzz" was beginning to wear off, Jeff had driven over to an older friend's apartment, where booze was always available, any hour of the day or night. Jeff downed three or four bourbon and gingers within about forty-five minutes.

By the time he got into the car to drive home, Jeff's "blood alcohol level" was slightly over .20—more than twice the amount at which the law judges drivers to be legally drunk. Unaware that this heavy intake of alcohol had impaired his ability to drive, Jeff raced down the road at a reckless pace, 25 miles (40 km) an hour over the speed limit.

Dangerously, he drifted across the center line of the road several times. Each time he was able to correct himself, but his reactions were slow and sluggish. Fortunately, at this hour, there was no oncoming traffic.

Ahead, however, was a curve sign that Jeff missed altogether. In seconds he was through the curve, across the other lane, and into the brush on the other side of the road. The bushes didn't slow the car at all. Fifty feet (15 m) further it hurtled, head on, into an oak tree at 60 miles (97 km) an hour.

The following is a split-second account of what happened then:

One-tenth of a second after impact, the front bumper and grillwork of Jeff's car collapsed, sending slivers of steel penetrating to a depth of 1½ inches (3.8 cm) into the tree. A tenth of a second later, the hood rose, crumpled, and smacked into the windshield. The fenders smashed into the tree, forcing the rear parts out over the front doors. Jeff's body moved forward at the vehicle's original speed. (At twenty times the normal force of gravity, his body weighed the equivalent of 3,200 pounds, or 1,450 kg.) His legs, ramrod straight, snapped at the knee joints.

Three-tenths of a second after impact, Jeff's body was off the seat, torso upright. The plastic and steel frame of the steering wheel began to bend under his horror-frozen grip. His head was now inches from the sun visor, and his chest was just above the steering column. By the next tenth of a second, the first 2 feet (.6 m) of the car had been demolished, as the half-ton motor block smashed into the tree with terrifying force. The car was now traveling at about 35 miles (56 km) per hour, but Jeff's body was still moving forward at 55 miles (89 km) per hour.

One half-second into the crash, Jeff's tightly clenched hands bent the steering column into an almost vertical position. The momentum impaled him on the steering shaft. Jagged steel punctured a lung and intercostal arteries. Blood spurted into his lungs as he gasped for breath.

At six-tenths of a second after impact, the brake pedal tore loose from the floor boards, and Jeff's feet were ripped from his tightly laced shoes. The car's chassis bent in the middle, shearing body bolts. The rear of the car, thrown upward at the instant of collision, began its downward fall, spinning wheels digging into the ground. Jeff's head sledgehammered into the windshield with such violence that his forehead was gashed open 2 inches, (5 cm) down the center.

At seven-tenths of a second, the entire writhing body of the car was forced out of shape. Hinges tore, and the doors sprang open. In one last convulsion, the seat rammed forward. Jeff remained pinned against the steering shaft. Blood poured from his mouth.

In less than three-quarters of a second, Jeff was dead.

Jeff is not a fictional character. He was a real person who died in precisely such an accident in southern Maryland in April 1982. Sadly, dozens of American teenagers are killed *daily* all across the nation in such senseless, preventable tragedies; hundreds more are injured, many crippled or scarred for life.

Half of all such accidents are alcohol or drug-related.

2
Shocking Statistics

In December 1981, an Air Florida jetliner took off from National Airport in Washington, D.C., in the midst of a light snowfall. Its wings and fuselage laden with encrusted ice, the plane labored to clear the runway, was airborne for only a few seconds, then crashed into the 14th Street Bridge, less than a mile (1.6 km) from the runway. The liner plummeted through a layer of ice covering the Potomac River and sank to the bottom. Seventy-eight persons, including the pilots and crew, were killed.

The crash made headlines across the nation and around the world. It was featured on network news programs for several nights running.

But on the same day as that plane crash—and every day of the year, for that matter—approximately as many people were killed in alcohol- or drug-related vehicular accidents in the United States, and there was little or no notice of it in the national news media. Yet the staggering and gruesome statistics that document the nation's roadway slaughter should command the attention of every citizen, because such traffic accidents are one of the country's leading causes of death, especially among young people, year after year.

[5]

Here are some of the sobering statistics:

■ In 1981, 49,125 people were killed in traffic accidents in the United States. The year before, 51,077 had been killed. This averages out to more than 130 deaths a day. About as many Americans die on U.S. roads every year as were killed during the entire Vietnam War.

■ Each year, approximately 3.5 million people are injured in over 800,000 vehicular crashes.

■ The total bill for all this carnage adds up to close to $35 billion a year.

About half of all this death and destruction was caused by drunk drivers, according to a 1982 congressional report called "Driver Safety," prepared for the Committee on Commerce, Science and Transportation by the National Highway Traffic Safety Administration. The report also cited that "accidents involving drunk drivers cost our society up to $24 billion each year in medical, rehabilitation, and insurance costs, property damage, lost work income and tax revenues, as well as police and emergency vehicle services."

Here are some further figures compiled by the National Highway Traffic Safety Administration:

■ On an average weekend night, one out of every ten drivers on the road is drunk. In fact, 80 percent of all fatal alcohol-related auto crashes occur between 8:00 P.M. and 8:00 A.M.

■ 65 percent of drivers who kill themselves in single-car wrecks are drunk.

■ One out of every two Americans will be involved in an alcohol-related auto crash in his or her lifetime.

For young Americans, the statistics are even more frightening. The number one cause of death among American teenagers is motor vehicle accidents, and more than half

Police survey the wreckage of an automobile that crashed into an embankment off a highway in New York. Of the four passengers in the car, all teenagers, only one, the driver, survived. The young man was later charged with driving while intoxicated.

of these accidents are caused by drunk drivers. The Insurance Institute for Highway Safety, an organization dedicated to reducing the losses resulting from highway accidents, says that "nearly half of all deaths of teenagers sixteen to nineteen years old are the result of motor vehicle crashes. Motor vehicles account for higher proportions of the deaths of sixteen-, seventeen-, eighteen-, and nineteen-year-olds than for any other age."

In one recent year, the institute found that "43 percent of the deaths of sixteen- to nineteen-year-olds (44 percent of male deaths and 42 percent of female deaths) were due to motor vehicle crashes." Further, "this age group, which was 8 percent of the population, sustained 17 percent of all motor vehicle related fatalities."

According to an institute study, "the teen years are the most treacherous ones on the highway, and the age of eighteen is particularly critical. More deaths per licensed driver were associated with the crashes of eighteen-year-olds than with any other age."

When depicted graphically, the statistics for almost every aspect of the teen driver problem jut up in towering peaks when compared with the pattern for the entire driver population—not only for teenaged drivers themselves but also for passengers in their vehicles, for occupants of other vehicles into which they crash, and for non-occupants such as pedestrians. "More than 60 percent of the passenger vehicle related deaths of sixteen- and seventeen-year-olds, about one-third of the deaths of fifteen-year-olds, one-quarter of the deaths of fourteen-year-olds, and smaller but appreciable proportions of the deaths of persons of other ages from infancy through late adulthood, resulted from sixteen- and seventeen-year-olds driving passenger vehicles," said the report.

Thus, the study emphasized, "When teenagers drive, they not only have a very high fatality rate themselves, but also contribute substantially to the deaths of others. . . . The majority of fatally injured teenaged passengers sustain [their] injuries in vehicles driven by teenagers."

In the year of the institute's study (1978), there were 4,198 deaths in crashes involving drivers sixteen and seventeen years old. The young drivers themselves accounted for 1,344 of those deaths, and 1,307 of their passengers died. The other fatalities were occupants in other vehicles with which the teen drivers collided and nonoccupants (motorcyclists, pedalcyclists, and pedestrians). Taken together, this accounts for 10 percent of the deaths that occurred in crashes involving a passenger vehicle in 1978. In addition, the report says that teenage boys have much higher rates of driver involvement in fatal crashes than teenage girls. For boys, the rate peaks at eighteen, whereas for girls it is highest at age sixteen.

Says U.S. Senator Claiborne Pell of Rhode Island, one of the nation's leading crusaders against drunk driving: "In the sixteen to twenty-four age group, alcohol is responsible for 8,000 highway deaths each year, and causes an additional 40,000 young people to be injured, many of them crippled or impaired for life."

The rise in alcohol-related accidents involving teenagers seems to be directly tied to another whole book of statistics, one pointing to the fact that teenagers are drinking more and at an earlier age than ever before. The National Institute on Alcohol Abuse and Alcoholism (NIAAA) says, "every indicator and every statistic available to us indicates an increase in the consumption of alcohol by young people. Our data indicate that young people are drinking sooner, more often, and in greater quantities than in the past." Adds psychologist Dr. William Rader, "More kids are drinking and drinking more often today than any other generation in the history of our country."

[9]

It is difficult to pinpoint, on a national scale, just how much this problem has grown in recent years, but the institute gained some enlightening information through two national surveys of high school populations conducted by the Research Triangle Institute, one in 1974 and the second in 1978. According to these studies, 30 percent of the respondents to the 1978 survey of tenth-through twelfth-graders stated that they had drunk enough to feel a little high or light-headed once a month or more in the last year, and 22 percent stated that they had been drunk or very, very high once a month or more. The 1974 survey, which reported on seventh- through twelfth-graders, provided evidence that experimenting with drinking alcohol begins early. More than half of the seventh-graders stated that they had taken at least one drink during the previous year.

Differences exist between the drinking patterns of boys and girls, although these differences appear to be diminishing. According to the 1978 survey, boys still drink more and in greater quantities than girls. For example, in the 1974 and 1978 surveys, approximately two out of three adolescent female drinkers were classified as drinking moderately or less. On the other hand, approximately one out of two adolescent male drinkers was classified as drinking moderately or less. Only 1 percent of the respondents to the 1978 survey stated that drinking had been a considerable or serious problem for them during the past year. But 23 percent had driven often after having had a "good bit to drink." The institute also said that the quantity of alcohol teenagers were drinking had increased overall from 1965 to 1975.

The National Association of Independent Insurers says, "Use of alcohol and drugs, particularly marijuana, is widespread among American teenagers." A 1981 survey by the University of Michigan found that over 92 percent of high school seniors had used alcohol at some time. More than 70 percent had used it in the previous month, and 6 percent used alcohol on a daily basis. A steady increase both in the overall use of alcohol and in its frequency of use among high school students has also been reported in several surveys conducted by the National Commission on Marijuana and Drug Abuse, the Addiction Research Foundation of Ontario, Canada, and local authorities in California and Florida.

The survey also discovered that 66 percent of high school seniors admitted to use of an illicit drug at some time. Fifty-nine percent of 1981 seniors had used marijuana, 31 percent in the previous month and 7 percent on a daily basis.

According to all the surveys, beer is the beverage most preferred by teenage drinkers, especially among males. In the National Institute on Alcohol Abuse and Alcoholism study, beer drinking at least once a week was reported by 10 percent of seventh-grade boys and 42 percent of twelfth-grade boys. Generally, the quantity of alcohol consumed at any one time by both boys and girls increased with grade level. The surveys have also indicated that young people have become significant users of the sweet, fruit-flavored wines since mass marketing of the wines began in the late 1960s.

In a nationwide study reported by the Distilled Spirits Council of the United States (DISCUS), it was found that teenagers who admitted to periodic drinking were just as likely to do well in school and take part in out-of-school activities as others. Those who reported that they did drink said they did it in a variety of places, but most frequently at a friend's home. Drinking was also said to take place at parks, beaches, or other outdoor places; at bars or restaurants; at school functions; or at drive-in movies.

How do all these statistics—the ones referring to an increase in teenage traffic accident fatalities and those relating to increases in teenage drinking—merge? Obviously, it is much more than coincidence that both sets of figures have been on the rise in recent years. One way to relate the two is to take a look at a special research report prepared by Leon S. Robertson of Yale University with the support of the Insurance Institute for Highway Safety.

Robertson's results included the following: "Only 75 percent of children born alive in 1900 in the United States reached their twentieth birthdays; by 1950, this figure was higher than 95 percent. The trend in death rate continued downward for younger children in the third quarter of the century, but it reversed among teenagers and young adults. At its historic low point in 1961–62, the death rate of persons fifteen to twenty-four years old was 10 per 10,000; by 1969–73, it had increasd to 13 per 10,000." Robertson attributed this shocking rise to the increase in motor vehicle accidents.

"Motor vehicles accounted for 38 percent of all deaths of persons fifteen to nineteen years old and 51 percent of their injury deaths in 1975," he said. "Half of permanent disability associated with traumatic injury to the spinal cord also occurs in or by motor vehicles—about the same proportion as deaths from injury."

"For the past seventy-five years, there has been a remarkable increase in the life expectancy of people in this country with one notable exception," adds Dr. Morris E. Chafetz, president of the Health Education Foundation. "Between the ages of sixteen and twenty-four, the life expectancy has dropped to what it was twenty years ago. Seventy-five percent of deaths in that age group are due to car accidents attributed to excess use of alcohol or drugs."

Statistics do not lie. Teenage drinking is on the rise. Teenage motor vehicle accidents causing death and serious injury are on the rise. These two indisputable facts are directly—and disastrously—related.

[12]

3
Why Drivers Drink

"When the walls are closing in on me—you know, when your parents are preaching at you all the time, maybe you've had a run-in at school, or your girl is giving you a hard time—that's when I like to have a few beers and then go for a drive," says "Curt," a seventeen-year-old Missouri high school junior.

"When I get behind the wheel of that car and mash the accelerator down, especially if I have a nice buzz-on, I get a feeling of power, of importance. I forget about all my frustrations, and it seems the faster I go, the more risks I take, the better I feel about it. I guess," Curt reflects, "if you stop to analyze it, it's crazy. All I can tell you is, if I have troubles, the combination of beer and speed seems to work for me. I love it."

Explains Morris Chafetz of the Health Education Foundation: "Drinking is a mechanism used by teenagers to cope with anxiety, frustration, and conflict."

But this is only one of many reasons why teenagers are drinking more alcohol today than ever before, drinking it more frequently, smoking more, and taking more drugs. What are some of the other reasons?

"I drink to relax," says John, an eighteen-year-old senior from Georgia. "Let's face it, I'm not the best-

[13]

looking guy in the world, and I feel funny talking to girls if I haven't had anything to drink. But after I get a glow on, I seem to loosen up. I do things I wouldn't ordinarily do if I were sober. I'm a lot more comfortable and confident."

Indeed, this tendency to shed inhibitions seems to be one of the more popular reasons teenagers drink, especially among boys. Says Jean Rosenblatt, author of a research report on teenage drinking: "Since alcohol reduces inhibitions [by shutting down certain brain impulses], it is not surprising that awkward, insecure teenagers, worried about their appearance and their effect on the opposite sex, might seek out its [alcohol's] relaxing effects."

Peer pressure is another leading cause of teenage drinking. According to a report issued by the National Association of Independent Insurers, "One of the strongest influences on an individual teen's decision to use or not use alcohol or drugs is the use of these substances by friends."

Adds a spokesperson for the National Institute on Alcohol Abuse and Alcoholism: "Peer influences become increasingly important during the teenage years, and peers seem to have a strong immediate impact on specific drinking episodes and, possibly, on experimental drinking. During these times, peers may not only provide a model for certain kinds of drinking, but also influence drinking simply by making alcohol more available to other youths."

Consider the case of "Tony," a sixteen-year-old resident of New Jersey: "When you're cruising around with the guys, you feel like a jerk if all of them are chugging beer and you're not. If you don't go along with them, you're not accepted in the crowd. The word gets around that you're a square." And, adds seventeen-year-old "Julie," a Detroit high school student: "It just felt like you were missing out on a lot of fun if you didn't join in."

"Teenage girls may be especially susceptible to male peer pressure," says Jean Rosenblatt. Researchers have found that girls were influenced by the drinking and drug-use patterns of boy friends more often than boys were influenced by girl friends' drug use.

Among college students, young women were likely to be "turned on" for the first time to alcohol, marijuana, and other drugs by young men, while the men were more likely to be given drugs and alcohol by other men. And while 70 percent of the men bought their own alcohol and drugs, only 11 percent of the young women did, according to one detailed study made in Walla Walla County, Washington.

Rosenblatt reported that teenage girls drink for the same reasons teenage boys do. "Girls who abuse alcohol usually have extremely low self-esteem, and their drinking often contributes to problems that reinforce their feelings of worthlessness." Marian Sandmaier, author of *The Invisible Alcoholics: Women and Alcohol Abuse,* adds: "Thousands [of young women] are drinking to the point where it is interfering with their schoolwork, damaging relationships with family and friends, contributing to unwanted sexual encounters and sometimes pregnancies, causing accidents and arrests, and generally undermining their emotional and physical health."

Many young people turn to alcohol as a means of expressing their anger at what they believe is too strict authority, usually administered by parents. Says one psychologist: "They experiment with different life-styles, choice of friends, relationships with the opposite sex, values often quite different from their parents'. Their need for experimentation is so strong that restrictions placed on them by parents are viewed as a lack of trust in them. They may feel so, even when they know inside that some of their actions are wrong or dangerous. The result sometimes shows itself in rebellious behavior."

Teenagers also complain that they are expected to

[15]

behave as adults in discharging certain responsibilities, yet remain children and be restricted from activities their parents think they are not ready for, such as drinking. Young people do tend to receive dual messages about drinking. The media portray drinking as highly desirable and glamorous "adult" behavior. Parents, on the other hand, often demand that their teenage children behave in an "adult" manner while forbidding them to drink. These mixed messages, say psychologists, tend to confuse teenagers, who are struggling with their own feelings about growing up. Therefore, some youths may consume alcohol as a means of claiming adult status; others may seize on drinking as a way of striking out against parents or other authority figures.

Taking this a step further, Jerry and Jan Lazar, coauthors of a report called "Youthful Drunk Drivers: A Mushrooming Crisis," noted: "The typical teenager begins drinking as a social phenomenon heavily influenced by a desire to be 'grown up.' It has been frequently pointed out that the socialization process tends to value drinking and encourages it through the prevalence of 'kiddie cocktails,' 'Shirley Temples,' and a wide range of simulated drinking behaviors. Sweet alcoholic drinks are condoned, thus equating drinks with candy in the minds of many children. This process, coupled with the frequent exposure of children to adult drinking behavior, including the cocktail party, the predinner drinks, and an assortment of other examples, would seem to have a strong impact on impressionable minds.

"The behavior of 'having a drink' is seen as desirable, as friendly, as a way to make one feel better, and, most dangerous of all, as an expected part of adult behavior in many parts of American society. Since it is a well-established fact that people learn by imitation, is it any wonder that children learn early and well that drinking is the 'in' thing to do?"

[16]

The Lazar report tied this phenomenon directly to the teenage drunk-driving problem by stating: "Teenagers who live with parents are more likely than any other age group to be drinking directly in their cars. They are too young, or at least a part of any group is likely to be too young, to drink in public. The tendency to drink in the car, or to drink while driving, is a predictable result of a society which tacitly, or openly in many cases, condones the drinking but forbids the use of an appropriate setting in which to drink. Circumstances have conspired to put the teenager, alcohol, and cars together in an explosive combination."

According to most experts, the majority of teenagers start drinking at home with their families, on special occasions and holidays. They enter adolescence with an impression of about thirteen years standing that most people, including their parents, enjoy social drinking and that moderate drinking is not usually harmful. After such early encouragement, teenagers find confusing and hypocritical the attitude of parents who scold them for drinking with friends their own age.

Parents have a strong effect on their children's future drinking behavior, both directly and indirectly. According to one NIAAA study: "As a specific influence, the parent's own drinking behavior provides a role model for his or her youngsters. Studies show that parents who abstain are likely to have youngsters who abstain during adolescence, and those who drink are likely to have children who drink. Drinking style is also important; parents who drink in a light or moderate fashion tend to rear offspring who also drink in a problem-free manner. However, since parents who abstain provide no role model for light or moderate, they may find that their children tend to drink heavily."

A number of teens drink, in part, because they believe it is a harmless activity. Reports the National Association of Independent Insurers: "The reasons teens give for using alcohol or drugs are similar to the reasons cited by adults, such as escapism or rebellion. But an important reason for the popularity of alcohol and marijuana among teens is that few think there is any harm in having a few drinks or in experimental or occasional use of marijuana.

"The common form of alcohol use among teens is occasional 'binge' drinking. The most common time and place for smoking marijuana is whenever or wherever teens hang out; before school, between classes, after school, at friends' houses when parents are out, while driving back and forth to school, or just joy-riding."

Stress has also been cited as a key factor both in teenage drinking and in driving while drinking. In an article entitled "Alcohol and Other Drugs Related to Young Drivers' Traffic Accident Involvement," written by Paul C. Whitehead and Roberta G. Gerrence for the *Journal of Safety Research,* the authors stated: "The peak in the collision rate at the ages of eighteen and nineteen may also be related to the numerous stressful life changes occurring during this period. These include graduating from school, moving away from home, deciding about employment, and, in the past, military draft. In any case, the available evidence indicates that social factors, rather than driving experience, condition of vehicle, or reporting practices, account for most of the excessive rates of collisions among young drivers."

Just how widespread is the drinking phenomenon among teens in the United States? This is difficult to pinpoint exactly, but a report published by NIAAA offers some insight. "America is a drinking society," the report notes. "At least two-thirds of the adult population drink, some regularly and some occasionally. Alcohol is woven into the pattern of American life as an integral part of many social functions, such as weddings, holiday festivities, and the cocktail hour.

[18]

"Surprising and even dismaying as it may be to many adults, drinking is nearly as widespread among American youth as among their parents. . . . Approximately one-fifth of high school students admit to being intoxicated at least once a month.

"What are the reasons for alcohol use by teenagers, and why do some youth abuse alcohol? Unraveling the answers is more complicated than one might suppose," the report continues. "It is now recognized that alcohol-related behavior is complex. A teenager's choice of whether to drink or not to drink, and how to drink, results from a complicated mix of feelings and values arising from personal, social, family, religious, and other factors."

Whatever the causes of youthful drinking, over the past decade both adults and young people have become more accepting of alcohol use by the young, according to results of the Purdue Opinion Panel and a Louis Harris poll on drinking attitudes. Says Dr. Gerald Globetti, a University of Alabama sociologist, "Sooner or later, all young people in our society are faced with the inevitable decision to drink or not to drink. Three-fourths of them will make this decision and use alcohol before they are legally entitled—one-third on a regular basis, while 5 to 10 percent will experience serious complications as a result of drinking, and one in twelve will go on to become an adult problem drinker or an alcoholic."

Many sociologists contend that "a few episodes of intoxication," especially among older teens, may signal only an experimental stage in the growing-up process. For them, drinking is one of many behaviors being tried. During this time in their development, adolescents are building a repertoire of adult behaviors—learning to drive an automobile, conduct "steady" relationships, and handle job responsibilities. Within this context, drinking is not an isolated event but, instead, part of a normal transition into adulthood.

[19]

Yet experts say this early experimentation with alcohol, combined with the fact that most teenagers also are learning to drive during the same period and are relatively inexperienced at both drinking and driving, can add up to a dangerous situation on the highways. "What they don't realize," says one traffic expert, "is that when they drink and drive, each of them becomes, in effect, a speeding bomb on the highway—ready to explode at the next curve or bump in the road."

4
The Sobering Effects

Late one night in the summer of 1982, a state policeman in Richmond, Virginia, noticed a car barely moving on the highway. He trailed the car, which was also weaving slightly, for a short distance and then flashed his blue lights, signaling the driver to pull over to the side of the road.

"Young lady," the officer said to the eighteen-year-old, "do you have any idea how fast you were going?"

Through glazed eyes, she looked at him blankly and slowly shook her head.

"You were doing 5 miles [8 km] per hour in a zone where the minimum speed is 40 [64 km]," the officer said. "May I ask why you were driving so slow?"

"Because I'm bombed out of my mind," the girl replied.

Although this girl, who was subsequently convicted of a charge of driving while intoxicated and sentenced to participate in an alcohol-safety training program, knew that she had had too much to drink, she is the exception. Most young people are not aware of the harmful effects of alcohol and drugs on their systems. In fact, many, after a few drinks or after smoking marijuana, believe they can handle situations better than when they are

This car, driven by a drunken driver in Pennsylvania, first crashed into the rear of another car, then slammed into a utility pole.

straight. They can't. Alcohol directly impairs a person's judgment, coordination, perception, and sense of balance; and the more one drinks, the greater the impairment.

Actually, drinkers in general, and teenage drinkers in particular, know very little about the alcohol they consume or what it does to them. There are a lot of common myths and misconceptions concerning the subject.

Alcohol is the oldest mood-altering drug known to humankind. We know from archaeological evidence that wine and beer were used in the oldest civilizations and were in the diets of most primitive peoples.

Ethyl alcohol, or *ethanol,* which is the active ingredient in distilled spirits, wines, and beers, has the power to produce feelings of well-being and to induce sedation, intoxication, and unconsciousness. Ethanol also has the potential for producing toxic effects on the mind and body that can be dangerous or even fatal to the drinker.

Many people drink because they believe alcohol works as a stimulant. Actually, the reverse is true. Alcohol is classed pharmacologically as a depressant drug. The "high" feeling that sometimes results from drinking is achieved from the depressant effects of alcohol on the brain.

The rate at which alcohol is absorbed into the bloodstream and its effects on an individual are influenced by a number of factors. On the physical side, a person's weight, how fast he or she drinks, whether he or she has eaten, the person's drinking history and body chemistry, and the kind of beverage used, are all influential.

With body weight, for example, the more body muscle in relation to fat, the lower the blood alcohol concentration (BAC) from a given amount of liquor. In a 160-pound (73-kg) person, alcohol is burned at about the rate of one drink every two hours. However, the more rapidly an alcoholic beverage is ingested, the faster the peak blood alcohol level will be reached. This is because alco-

[23]

hol is metabolized, or burned up in the body, at a fairly constant rate. When a person drinks faster than the alcohol can be burned, the drug accumulates in the body, resulting in higher and higher levels of alcohol in the blood. Drinking at the rate of one drink every two hours will result in little, if any, accumulation of alcohol in the blood.

Food also has a direct affect on this accumulation. A person who drinks on an empty stomach, for instance, generally will become high or intoxicated much faster than one who has eaten. Eating while drinking retards the absorption of alcohol.

Body chemistry plays a part, too. Individuals with a long history of drinking develop tolerance, which means they require far more alcohol to get high than an inexperienced drinker. How quickly one becomes high, or how fast one sobers up, may also be influenced by such factors as anger, fear, stress, nausea, and the condition of the stomach tissues. In addition, the drinking situation and the drinker's mood, attitudes, and what the individual wants to happen or expects to happen based on previous drinking experiences all will contribute to drinking reactions.

A common misconception about the effects of alcohol, especially among teenagers, is the belief that beer and wine will not have as much effect as hard liquors. What teens often don't realize is that the significant ingredient in all these drinks is identical—alcohol. On the average, one shot of 80-proof whiskey, gin, or vodka is the same as a 4- or 5-ounce (113- or 142-g) glass of wine, or one 12-ounce (340-g) container of beer. Each has about 1/2 ounce (14 g) of alcohol.

The higher the concentration of alcohol in a drink, the more rapidly the alcohol is absorbed. The greater the volume of nonalcoholic substances such as water or cola, the more slowly the alcohol is absorbed. Thus, if two people of equal weight and experience drink Scotch, one with

[24]

water and one straight, the one drinking it straight is likely to get "high" faster.

How do different blood-alcohol levels affect behavior? The first consistent, noticeable changes in mood and behavior appear at BAC's of approximately 0.05, that is, one part alcohol to 2,000 parts blood, 1/20 of 1 percent, or 50 milligrams of alcohol per decaliter of blood. This level would result from a 160-pound (73-kg) person taking two drinks in an hour. If you weigh less than this, chances are alcohol has a greater effect on you, causing a higher BAC; if you weigh more, it has a lesser effect and produces a lower BAC.

At the 0.05 BAC level, thought, judgment, and restraint may be affected; a person may feel carefree and released from ordinary tensions and inhibitions. As more alcohol enters the blood, additional functions of the brain become impaired. At a level of 0.10 percent (one part alcohol to 1,000 parts blood), which, incidentally, is considered legally intoxicated in most states, voluntary motor actions—hand and arm movements, walking, and sometimes speech—become plainly clumsy. Often a person will slur his or her words in talking.

How much drinking does it take to reach this 0.10 level? In general, if a 150-pound (68-kg) person has five drinks of whiskey, five glasses of wine, or five cans of beer in one hour on an empty stomach, he or she is there. One-tenth of 1 percent of the blood content may not seem like much. Considering there are about 1½ gallons (5.7 liters) of blood in a 150-pound person's body, five drinks would amount to about a teaspoon of pure alcohol. Yet even this tiny percentage is enough to turn a good driver into a highway menace. Statistics show that drivers at 0.10 BAC are six or seven times more likely to have an accident than if their BAC were zero. And if the BAC gets up to 0.15 percent, their chances of crashing are twenty-five times greater!

At 0.20 percent BAC (one part alcohol to 500 parts

blood), the functioning of the entire motor area of the brain is measurably impaired. The part of the brain that guides emotional behavior is also affected. Common characteristics may include staggering or a desire to lie down. A person may easily be angered at this BAC level, become boisterous, or even cry. At 0.20 BAC, he or she is very drunk.

At a concentration of 0.30 (one part to 300), the deeper areas of the brain concerned with response to stimuli and understanding are dulled. At this level, a person is confused, or may lapse into a stupor. He or she has poor understanding of what is seen or heard. With a 0.40 or 0.50 BAC (one part to 250 or 200), the drinker will become unconscious. Still higher levels of alcohol in the blood block the centers of the brain that control breathing and heartbeat, and death occurs. This progression of effects is not unique to alcohol. It can be produced by other hypnotic-seductive drugs, such as barbiturates, ether, and chloral hydrate.

What are some of the effects of alcohol on the senses? Even low doses of alcohol will reduce sensitivity to taste and odors. Alcohol has little effect on the sense of touch, but dulls sensitivity to pain. Sharpness of vision seems relatively unaffected by alcohol. However, a narrowing of the visual field, often called "tunnel vision," occurs, which may be particularly dangerous in automobile driving because of the fact that peripheral objects are often not seen.

Low doses of alcohol reduce resistance to glare so that the eye requires a longer time to readjust after exposure to bright lights. This can produce a period of relative blindness that can be hazardous for driving. Alcohol also impairs the ability to discriminate between lights of different intensities. Sensitivity to certain colors, especially red, appears to decrease. When alcohol and marijuana are taken together, color vision—the ability to discriminate between green-yellow and red-yellow—also becomes impaired.

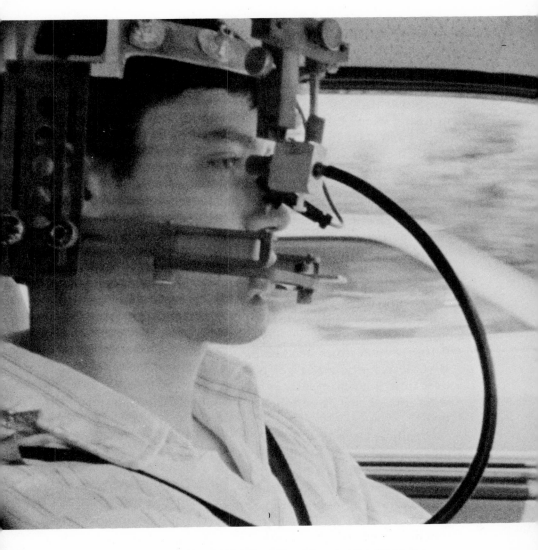

This odd-looking headgear was used in an Ohio University study on drunk driving. A television camera atop the apparatus recorded the driver's field of vision, and videotape was later used to analyze the visual effects of different levels of alcohol.

Driving simulator and road-test studies have shown that certain sensory and mental functions necessary for good driving are impaired by alcohol and marijuana use. These include sustained attention, decision-reaction time for passing, estimating time required for passing, ability to stop at traffic lights or signs, ability to stay in a lane, tracking where cars are in other lanes, and judgment on brake and start time.

Alcohol also affects motor performance. Tests of muscular control or coordination show that intoxicating doses of alcohol impair most types of performance. For example, drinking increases swaying, especially if the eyes are closed. Alcohol impairs neuromuscular (motor) coordination needed for such driving tasks as shifting gears. It also has an adverse effect on attention, memory, and conceptual processes. For instance, reaction time, an indicator of attention, is measured by the rapidity with which a person makes a simple movement, such as pressing a button in response to a sound or visual signal. Tests have shown that between blood-alcohol levels of 0.08 and 0.10, reaction times become measurably slower. Higher BAC levels produce larger performance failures. Reaction time is even greater when attention is divided, as when the person is simultaneously engaged in another task.

Significant loss of memory occurs with acute doses of alcohol and may develop into "blackouts" involving amnesia without loss of consciousness. In fact, memory-storage processes are particularly disrupted by alcohol.

A common myth regarding drinking is that it improves sexual activity. To the contrary, however, tests have consistently revealed that large doses of alcohol frustrate sexual performance. Studies of alcoholics have revealed that their sex lives were disturbed or ineffectual.

The effects of alcohol on sleep are known to anyone who has gone to bed exhausted after having had too much to drink, only to toss and turn and awaken the following morning feeling headachy and fatigued. Taking several drinks before bedtime has been found to decrease the amount of REM (rapid eye movement), or dreaming, while asleep. Some of the consequences of being deprived of REM sleep are impaired concentration and memory, as well as anxiety, tiredness, and irritability.

The combination of alcohol with drugs such as sleeping pills, tranquilizers, or cold tablets—all of which may include narcotics, barbiturates, and other hypnotic-sedative drugs plus antihistamines and volatile solvents—can grossly exaggerate the usual responses expected from alcohol or from a drug alone. This is due to the additive or combined effects exerted by alcohol and the other drugs on the central nervous system. Alcohol and barbiturates, when combined, multiply each other's effect. Doctors warn that taking drugs and alcohol together is very dangerous and may result in serious injury or even death.

Some of the greatest myths concerning alcohol revolve around quick ways to sober up. How many times have you heard someone say to a person who has had too much to drink, "Take a cold shower," or "Drink some black coffee." In truth, neither of these "remedies" has any effect.

Just as the speed of alcohol absorption affects the rate at which one becomes intoxicated, the speed at which the alcohol is metabolized affects the rate at which one becomes sober again. Once in the bloodstream and carried throughout the body, alcohol undergoes metabolic changes and is eventually reduced to carbon dioxide and water. Most of these complex processes take place in the liver, although from 2 to 5 percent of the alcohol is excreted chemically unchanged in urine, breath, and sweat.

The truth is, only time can sober up an intoxicated person. It takes about one hour for the body to dispose of an ounce (28 g) of whiskey or a single can of beer.

[29]

Likewise, there are many common myths about hangovers—the morning-after misery of fatigue, nausea, upset stomach, anxiety, and headache. The hangover is unpleasant but rarely dangerous. Although it has been blamed on mixing different types of drinks, a hangover can be produced by any alcoholic beverage, or by pure alcohol. The exact cause is unknown. However, it is not true that such remedies as coffee, raw eggs, oysters, vitamins, more drinks, or such drugs as barbiturates or amphetamines, will quickly dispel the bad effects of a hangover. Doctors usually prescribe aspirin, bed rest, and solid food as soon as possible. Again, time is the only proven remedy.

What are the long-term effects of alcohol on the body? Drinking in small quantities apparently does not seriously harm the body. But, when taken in large amounts over long periods of time, alcohol can prove disastrous, reducing both the quality and length of life. Damage to the heart, brain, liver, and other major organs may result.

Prolonged heavy drinking has long been known to be connected with various types of muscle diseases and tremors. One essential muscle affected by alcohol is the heart. Some research indicates that alcohol is toxic to the heart.

But it is diseases of the liver that are most commonly associated with heavy drinking. Cirrhosis of the liver occurs about eight times as often among alcoholics as among nonalcoholics. Recent studies have also shown that among heavy consumers of alcohol, the death rates from cancers of the mouth and pharynx, larynx, esophagus, liver, and lung are also increased. This effect is compounded when the drinker also smokes.

Heavy drinking over many years may result in serious mental disorders or permanent, irreversible damage to the brain or peripheral nervous system. Mental functions such as memory, judgment, and learning ability can deteriorate severely, and an individual's personality structure and grasp on reality may disintegrate as well.

How does all this relate to the teenage drunk-driving problem? A major contributing factor to the high incidence of vehicular accidents caused by teenagers who have been drinking, in relation to other groups, is that young people appear to have accidents at lower blood-alcohol concentrations than older drivers. Experts believe this occurs because teenagers are relatively inexperienced both in drinking and driving.

Says NIAAA: "Because most teenagers learn to drive when they are sixteen to seventeen years old, and start drinking just a year or so before that, the combined inexperience seems to encourage greater risk taking." A report issued by the Distilled Spirits Council of the United States cites: "To combine inexperienced drinking with inexperienced driving is courting trouble. The last thing learned is the first forgotten in an emergency. Driving in today's vehicles in today's traffic calls for split-second decisions. Such decisions are made more repeatedly and more successfully by adults who have miles and years of experience upon which to draw. New drivers of any age have not had enough experience for judgments to be reliable.

"New drinkers do not have enough experience to know their own personal responses to even one drink. They have neither built up an awareness of their tolerance, nor learned that the effect of alcohol is more potent on an empty stomach, that it is compounded when mixed with prescription or other drugs, that emotional factors such as anger and physical factors such as fatigue can alter one's tolerance."

Some additional factors that authorities believe lead to more accidents by drinking teenagers than by other age groups are noted in the Lazar report: "The younger the drinkers, the less likely they are to recognize personal limits in either alcohol consumption or driving skills; thus they are less able to correctly cope with the effects of alcohol. They are also more likely to be in situations where peer pressure leads to excess.

"By virtue of their age, they are likely to be forced to be home at a prescribed time; therefore, they will be driving without having the requisite time to achieve sobriety. These drinkers do not have the advantage of being able to stay out until the alcohol has an opportunity to be eliminated from their systems.

"The tendency to drink in the car or to drink while driving," summarizes the Lazar report, "is a predictable result of a society that tacitly (or openly in many cases) condones the drinking, but forbids the use of an appropriate setting in which to drink."

In brief, the Lazar report lists the following factors contributing to the problem:

■ availability of automobiles to teenagers sixteen and above
■ unstructured time without adult supervision
■ ability to purchase or obtain alcohol and having the money to do so
■ social tolerance of intoxication
■ adult example of drinking
■ inexperience at drinking and driving.

Thus, the report's authors comment: "Circumstances have conspired to put the teenager, alcohol, and cars together in an explosive combination. The question now becomes, What can society realistically do to defuse the bombed teenager?"

5
Driving Stoned

One a.m. The 1980 Chrysler Le Baron raced dangerously over the bumpy, winding two-lane road in rural DeLand, Florida. The driver, a seventeen-year-old boy named Gary, and Patrick, his sixteen-year-old passenger friend, laughed nervously as the speeding auto weaved back and forth across the center line. Suddenly, a curve sign loomed in the high-beam headlights, warning that the maximum safe speed was 25 miles (40 km) per hour. "Watch it, Gary," Patrick yelled.

Gary slammed on the brakes, but it was too late. The car went skidding sideways off the road. It leaped across a narrow ditch, tore up more than 150 feet (40 m) of lawn and flowers, and then slammed, passenger side, into a telegraph pole. Neither boy had his seat belt on. Miraculously, Gary emerged from the crash with only a bloodied forehead. Patrick was less fortunate. He bore the full brunt of the impact, which snapped his spinal cord, paralyzing him from the waist down.

Gary and Patrick were not drunk. They were stoned— intoxicated from smoking marijuana at a party they had left only a few minutes earlier.

"How fast were you going?" the investigating highway patrol officer asked Gary.

"No more than 40 miles [64 km] per hour," he answered.

The officer knew better. By estimating the length of the tire skids on the road, the torn up lawn and shrubbery, and the force with which the car had smashed into the pole, the officer estimated that Gary had to have been going at least 70 miles (113 km) per hour, perhaps even faster, when he reached the curve.

But he also knew from experience that Gary probably wasn't lying, because one of the effects of a marijuana "high" is a severe distortion of speed. Gary actually believed he was driving no faster than 40, when in reality he was going at nearly twice that speed.

This is one of the primary dangers of driving while under the influence of drugs, and it is a big factor in the growing annual rate of vehicular accidents caused by drivers stoned on "grass," methaqualone tablets, "speed," and, to a lesser extent, cocaine, LSD, "angel dust," and even heroin.

This rising roll of death and serious injury, especially among teenagers and caused by the combination of drugs and driving, is a relatively recent phenomenon. According to national surveys, in 1962 only about 4 percent of Americans aged eighteen to twenty-five had ever used marijuana. Yet, just seventeen years later, in 1979, a startling 35 percent of those in the same age group surveyed—more than one-third—reported having used marijuana within the past month. Statistics involving various other drugs are equally alarming.

The National Institute on Drug Abuse (NIDA) reports that 60 to 80 percent of marijuana users questioned in one survey said they sometimes drive while high on pot. A NIDA spokesperson calls it "a national epidemic among young people." In one nationwide survey, taken in 1979, one out of every nine high school seniors interviewed admitted that he or she smoked marijuana daily. This was almost twice the number who had reported using pot in another study undertaken just four years earlier.

In reference to methaqualone (Quaalude by trade name, or just "lude" to most users), experts estimate that young people in their teens or early twenties consumed more than one billion tablets in 1981 alone. This made it one of the most popular drugs, ranking second only to marijuana in overall use among the nation's youth.

It is difficult to assess accurately just what percentage of America's 50,000 per-year traffic deaths and 3.5 million traffic accident injuries are directly caused by drivers stoned on marijuana or other drug substances. One reason for this is that there is as yet no fully reliable means of measuring the intoxication level of stoned drivers, as there is with alcohol.

Nevertheless, authorities are convinced that the number is both high and rising. For example, one survey taken in the state of Washington disclosed that marijuana users have a 39 percent higher traffic accident and violation rate than nonusers. The National Association of Independent Insurers estimates that "Potentially, 40 percent of today's young adults drive while high on marijuana." When Quaaludes and other drugs, pills, tablets, and powders are included, it becomes obvious that the number of teenagers driving while stoned increases substantially.

Adding to the overall problem is the fact that more and more young people are combining drugs with alcohol. More teens are smoking marijuana "joints" while swilling hard liquor, wine, or beer; more are washing down "upper" and "downer" pills with beer or other alcoholic beverages.

In one study involving 1,271 college students in Vermont, it was found that 60 percent of those who used marijuana combined it with alcohol at least occasionally, and 39 percent said they did so at least half the time. Fourteen percent said they combined alcohol and mari-

[35]

juana at least once a week. More than 90 percent of those surveyed drove automobiles. In a 1975 study done in Boston, it was revealed that 9 percent of fatal car collisions were directly attributable to marijuana alone, and an additional 22 percent of the drivers had been using marijuana in combination with alcohol or other drugs.

The reason for the increasingly popular pastime of combining drugs and "booze" is that it achieves a faster "high." It also greatly increases the danger of accidents, because the combination of alcohol and drugs increases the effects of each substance on the user. Thus, a driver who has consumed both alcohol and marijuana or another drug is more than doubly dangerous when behind the wheel of a vehicle.

Says Hugh Alcott, project manager of the California Department of Corrections' Special Narcotics Section: "A lot of people who have had too much to drink and know their driving skill will be affected, smoke a joint 'so they can drive better.' They actually believe that marijuana acts as an antidote to the effects of alcohol. All the pot does, of course, is to make them *feel* they're driving better. In fact, their driving is far more impaired than if they'd used alcohol alone."

There is no real secret to why teenagers smoke marijuana or pop pills. The reasons are much the same as those given for drinking: to "feel good," "to loosen up," to get relief from tension, to express anger, and so on.

But a common problem among young drug users, not found as often among those who drink, is that they believe that while high on marijuana or other drugs, they still know what they are doing and are in control of the situation. Indeed, a great number of teens feel they can drive as well as always while under the influence of marijuana. Incredibly, some even believe that their senses and reactions are sharpened by the drug. Most users perceive marijuana as harmless.

[36]

Although drinking often creates a distinct "buzz" sensation, which teenagers can physically feel, drugs sometimes do not. It can be a different "high." Marijuana, for example, can lull drivers into an overly relaxed, "laid back" frame of mind that diminishes their realization of on-the-road hazards. The driver feels a false confidence that he or she can handle any situation. In addition, scores of detailed research studies have shown that normal "social doses" of marijuana are just as impairing to the driver as alcohol.

"The preponderance of evidence indicates that marijuana impairs skills performance and perceptual processes, including vision, attention, and tracking behavior—all important components of driving performance," says Dr. Herbert Moskowitz, a University of California research psychologist who is acknowledged as one of the nation's leading authorities on the effects of marijuana on drivers.

What are some of the specific effects of marijuana on a person's driving performance? The National Association of Independent Insurers gives results from more than fifty detailed studies on the subject:

■ *Sustained attention.* Many drivers surveyed during tests found they were "not as attentive" as when they had not used marijuana. Some reported feeling "dreamy." One said, "Sometimes you just fix your eyes on one center thing on the road." Many said they felt they had to concentrate harder while driving under the influence of drugs.

Said another driver: "Marijuana seems to shift a person's attention away from what is happening on the road. You tend to concentrate on your own thoughts, and these attention lapses may cause you to miss an important piece of information, such as a stop sign, stoplight, or a car entering an intersection."

[37]

■ *Decision-reaction time for passing, and estimating time required for passing.* A number of drivers tested while under the influence of marijuana stated they had difficulty with depth perceptions, especially when judging the speed and distance of oncoming cars while passing cars in their own lane. Several said that objects (including oncoming cars) seemed to be further away than they actually were. This sensation is particularly dangerous, especially on two-lane roads.

■ *Ability to stop at traffic lights or signs.* Failure to stop is one of the three most prevalent traffic violations of marijuana users. (The other two are reckless driving and failure to yield.) Many test respondees said they had run through stop signs because they had perceived them to be further away than they actually were.

■ *Ability to stay in a lane.* While some drivers reported they couldn't "drive straight," and recognized this, others who were seen weaving in traffic didn't know they were doing it.

■ *Tracking a moving vehicle.* A large percentage of tested drivers reported having trouble braking quickly when the situation called for it, or veering quickly to avoid a road hazard.

■ *Reacting to more than one stimulus requiring a reaction.* Here, the drivers being tested found it difficult to concentrate on multiple things. If they were concerned about how close they were to a car in front of them, for example, they were slow to react to another car pulling up on a side road. Their concentration levels were limited.

A California highway patrolman shows a drunk-driving suspect what he is required to do to pass a sobriety test.

■ *Memory and ability to process new input.* Interestingly, some drivers said they had trouble remembering where to get off the highway, or which prescribed side road to take, even if they were familiar with it. Some were thinking so hard about driving that they forgot everything except whatever was right in front of them.

Researchers also found that many marijuana users who were tested had reduced visual capacity. This was particularly true in night driving. Many reported having trouble adjusting to glare caused by oncoming car headlights. Some had trouble with dimensions. Said one driver: "The view from my windshield oftentimes appears to be nothing more than a flat movie screen in front of the car."

Other negative effects reported included difficulty in backing up or turning around, inability to feel one's foot on the accelerator, and becoming frightened to the point of paranoia in heavy traffic. As might be imagined, the larger the amounts of marijuana used, the more driving skills are diminished.

There is some evidence that teenagers are becoming more aware of the hazards of driving while under the influence of marijuana. Recently, the American Automobile Association Foundation for Traffic Safety published a survey of 5,500 students from one hundred high schools in sixteen states. All these students admitted to driving after using marijuana. More than half said that the drug had harmful effects on steering, braking, making decisions, reacting to any emergency, and responding correctly to traffic signs and signals. Two-thirds said that marijuana harmed their ability to stay in one lane; and nearly 72 percent said it harmed their ability to pay attention.

Yet, even with this recognition, many teenagers remain naive about the overall harmful effects. One area least understood is the lingering effects. Unlike alcohol, which leaves the body relatively fast, marijuana after-effects may last several hours or even days after use. Because THC (tetrahydrocannabinol, the active chemical in marijuana) is fat soluble, the effects of a single high may persist as long as twelve hours, and the residue THC may not be completely metabolized for a week. Further, while THC is still in the system, only a few puffs of another joint can quickly rekindle the high. Thus, many teenagers who may think that the negative effects have worn off, drive vehicles while still at least partially under the influence. This heightens the chances of an accident because the drivers are totally unaware that their driving skills may still be impaired.

While the problems of driving under the influence of marijuana are relatively new—the escalation of marijuana use has occurred mostly over the past two decades— the consequences are the same as they are for drivers drunk on alcohol. In this case, however, the highway menace is compounded by the fact that so many drug users are not aware that their getting stoned has any significant negative effect on their driving performance.

Warns the Drug Abuse Council: "Driving an automobile under the influence of any mood-altering drug, including marijuana, is dangerous. It is particularly dangerous in heavy traffic where the driver must make many rapid decisions simultaneously. Even if marijuana possession is not a crime, as in some states, driving while intoxicated on marijuana or any other drug is illegal."

6
The Outrage

Of every 2,000 drunk drivers in America, only one is arrested. Even then the chances of receiving a serious penalty are mathematically insignificant. Annually, thousands of drunk drivers who are caught get off free, while the great majority of others apprehended are released with little more than a brief lecture by a judge, or a token slap on the wrist in the form of a light fine and a suspended jail sentence. Repeat offenders—including many who have killed or maimed people because of their impaired driving—plea-bargain with the courts to have jail sentences greatly reduced or suspended. Most of the nation's drunk drivers are back on the streets and highways within hours of a conviction. An alarming number kill and maim again.

Why? Because until recently, the nation has been appallingly apathetic about what many experts call the number-one national disaster—death on the highways.

Such apathy among the general population, and leniency in courtrooms toward offenders, can be attributed in part to human nature. Most of us drink, and a great percentage of us drive after drinking. Many members of juries sitting on drunk-driving cases drink and drive, so naturally they can sympathize with the person

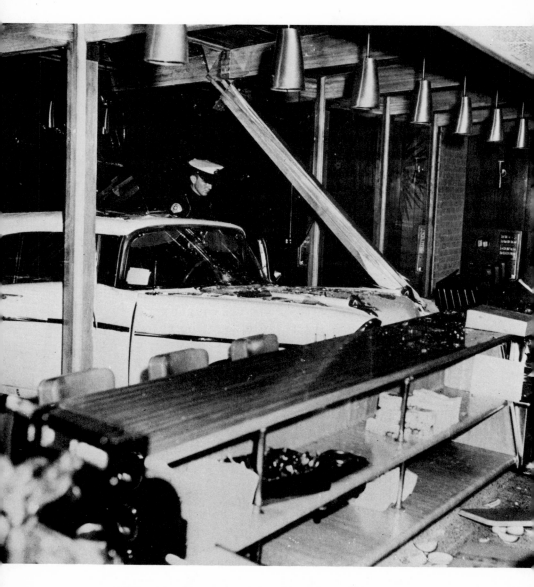

*This car, driven by a drunk driver, crashed into
the plate glass window of a restaurant in California.*

on trial. Many judges, too, drink and drive, which may explain why they often mete out such light sentences to offenders.

Another reason for the apathy may be the fact that drunk-driving deaths and injuries are so commonplace today, they are taken for granted. They are not given the media attention that other, more spectacular causes of death command. Vehicular crashes get buried under the sheer volume of their enormous statistics, and often rate only a brief mention on the back pages of newspapers.

This national attitude of turning one's head the other way regarding alcohol-related carnage on the highways caused Los Angeles Deputy District Attorney Joseph Siler to comment: "If we measured absolute levels of danger, we would fear drunk drivers more than all other criminals added together because they kill about 25,000 people a year, where homicides number only about 20,000. Drunk drivers also injure more people, and injure them more seriously, than those who commit assaults with deadly weapons. They do more property damage than the forgers and burglars and robbers all added together.

"In Los Angeles, some 50,000 persons a year are prosecuted for drunk driving by the city attorney's office, but although their actions jeopardize lives and property, the worst punishment they face for a first offense is six months in jail or a $500 fine." And, Siler added, most receive much lighter sentences. The reason for this is often the loopholes in the laws and plea-bargaining by defense lawyers to get sentences and fines reduced.

But things are changing fast. As the number of alcohol- and drug-related deaths continue to increase, there is now a growing groundswell of outrage building across America. Tens of thousands of people from all walks of life are becoming irate at the useless slaughter being wrought on the nation's highways.

And their anger is being felt. In state after state across the land, organizations against drunk drivers are sprouting up, and the impact of this dynamic new force of public opinion is being felt in courthouses and state legislatures throughout the country.

Using their constitutionally guaranteed rights as citizens, these determined individuals and groups are banding together to seek ways to curb this mounting problem. They are lobbying state and national lawmakers, in an effort to enact tougher and harsher penalties for offenders. They are reaching out through community and regional education programs, aimed at informing teenagers, parents, and others of the dangers of drinking and driving.

An example of this powerful emerging movement is Mrs. Candy Lightner of Fair Oaks, California. At about 1:30 on Saturday afternoon, May 6, 1980, Lightner's thirteen-year-old daughter, Cari, and her friend, Carla, were walking along a bicycle path on their way to a church fair. Suddenly, Carla heard a thump and turned to ask Cari what had happened. All she saw were Cari's shoes. The girl had been struck by a hit-and-run driver and was thrown 125 feet (38 m). She died an hour later.

A few days later, police arrested a forty-seven-year-old man and charged him with felony hit-and-run and felony drunk driving. Lightner was shocked to learn that the man had two previous drunk-driving convictions on his record and only two days before the fatal accident had been arrested on a third drunk-driving charge, for which he had posted bail. Despite these previous incidents, the man had served a total of only two days in jail.

How, Lightner asked, could such a person be allowed to drive again? She was also stunned at the reaction of friends to the man's arrest. "They were coming up to me and saying, 'But for the grace of God, that could have been me who did that.' If Cari had been raped or murdered, nobody would have said that," Lightner said.

When Lightner told a deputy district attorney that she wanted the man's license revoked and him in jail before he killed someone else, the law officer said, "Good luck, lady. You're fighting an uphill battle."

This made Candy Lightner mad, fighting mad. "I wanted to kill," she remembers. Instead, she found a more positive way to vent her rage. "I became determined," she says, "to find some way to help keep drunk drivers off the road."

First, she started reading. She pored over volumes of the Vehicle Code and the Penal Code. She read and reread the anti–drunk-driving bills that had failed to pass in the California state legislature. She began attending court sessions and asking questions. No one could satisfactorily tell her why so many drunk drivers were let off with little or no punishment. "Everywhere I went," she says, "everyone wanted to blame everyone else. The legislators blamed the judges and vice versa. No one seemed concerned enough to do anything about it."

Lightner did, however. She took $10,000 in savings and $15,000 from her late daughter's life insurance fund and formed an organization called Mothers Against Drunk Driving, or MADD. The charter goals were simple—to reduce the number of deaths and injuries caused by drunk drivers and to offer support and services to the victims of drunk drivers.

One of her first objectives was to meet with then-California Governor Jerry Brown in the hope of getting him to appoint a state task force to examine the drunk-driving problem and recommend ways to solve it. She wanted to see tougher laws and penalties on the books.

Brown wouldn't see her, so Lightner took her crusade to the press. She armed herself with statistics and talked before any group that would listen, large or small. She got on radio and television talk shows. In October 1980, she went to Washington, D.C., and held a news conference. There, three members of the U.S. Congress went on record as favoring stiffer penalties for drunk drivers.

The grass-roots publicity campaign began to take effect. Lightner finally got in to see Governor Brown, and he agreed to appoint a task force to study the problem. Meanwhile, as word of her efforts spread, other mothers across the state joined forces. Chapters began to spring up, first in California, then in other states.

In Maryland, for example, a young woman named Cindy Lamb organized a chapter and later was appointed vice-president of MADD. Lamb's five-month-old daughter, Laura, was permanently paralyzed from the shoulders down when the car she was riding in was struck by a drunk driver. The man had fifty-six separate entries on his driving record, including three previous arrests for drunk driving.

After national television appearances by Lightner and others on such shows as "Today," "Good Morning America," and "The Phil Donahue Show," letters and calls came in from thousands of people who wanted to join the cause. With such growing support, MADD broadened its base, to work not only for stiffer penalties for drunk drivers but also to provide assistance for the victims of drunk drivers and promote education programs in the schools. Other current goals of MADD include:

■ Encouraging greater public awareness of how the judicial system works. MADD asks their members to monitor court proceedings. Says Lightner: "You very rarely see the family of a victim in court. All that most judges see is that maybe the defendant's family will go on welfare if the drunk driver goes to prison. No one sees what we go through, what a devastating effect this has on the family of the victim, emotionally and financially."

■ Soliciting members to write state and national legislators demanding that tougher laws be passed and enforced.

■ Encouraging members to form regional and state task forces to examine the problem area by area and recommend courses for corrective action.

■ Preparing instructions for members to counsel, speak in public, work the local press in areas, and appear on TV and radio talk shows. MADD has even prepared a "survivor's manual," a step-by-step guide that tells how to change the court system, how to testify, and so on.

MADD has gained tremendous momentum since its founding in 1980. As this book was being written, there were eighty-three chapters in twenty-nine states, and more new ones were being added every month.

MADD may now be the largest such organization in the country, but it is not the only one. Another group that has gained legions of members in recent years is called Remove Intoxicated Drivers-USA, RID for short. It has fifty-five chapters in twenty-nine states and continues to grow. And, says national coordinator Doris Aiken of New York, "This is a campaign that is not going to go away. The pendulum will not swing back. There is an endless supply of victims." RID's goals are similar to MADD's, except that RID emphasizes deterrence more than punishment and has as many nonvictims as victims for chapter heads.

One of the most encouraging signs in this war against drunk driving has been the recent formation of an organization called Students Against Drunk Drivers, or SADD. It began as a high school project in Wayland, Massachusetts, near Boston. There, 900 students signed "SADD contracts" with their parents, promising to call home at any hour when a sober ride home was not available. In return, the parents pledged to come and get them at any hour, anyplace, no questions asked, and no arguments at the time.

"Most of us are at the age when we're just getting our licenses, and as the kids get into their high school years, there's more pressure on them to drink," says Dana Fokos, vice-president of the Wayland SADD chapter. "Now is the time for them to get the idea that alcohol, teens, and autos are a deadly combination."

The SADD movement has four basic goals:

■ to save teenagers' lives and the lives of others;

■ to make students more aware of the problem of drinking and driving, and aware of the fact that it can become a very personal problem at times;

■ to develop and encourage peer counseling among students, in relation to alcohol use;

■ to increase public awareness of this problem, and to call for its prevention everywhere.

SADD is catching on, say its backers, because it has a different approach—teens talking with teens. "When parents tell students not to drink and drive, it's not as effective as when your own peers say that," says Wayland SADD member Lisa Ye. And, adds Wayland student advisor Bob Anastas: "The most important part of the program is where teenagers are influencing other teenagers—what we call positive peer pressure."

The SADD movement is catching on. Within a year of the start of the program at Wayland, a hundred other Massachusetts schools had organized chapters. Many other states report an active interest in SADD.

In Maryland, for example, two teenagers formed chapters in their schools after a close mutual friend of theirs was killed by an intoxicated driver. They have taken their cause public, with radio and TV appearances and articles in newspapers.

Another SADD group was started by Kim Ritchie of Fairfax County, Virginia, then a sophomore at W. T. Woodson High School. "What we are trying to do right now," Ritchie said in an address to Virginia state senators in Richmond in 1982, "is to create a peer pressure that says it's okay to say no to drinking. We want to let students know that there are friends behind them if they say no. If our efforts can save one life, it's worth it."

Ritchie says she was afraid she might be laughed out of school when she started her drive, which was after learning that one of her fellow classmates had been killed in an alcohol-related car crash. But within days, she had more than a thousand student signatures on a petition endorsing the SADD movement.

That the idea of campaigns by teenagers against drunk driving is catching on was further exemplified in Grand Rapids, Michigan. There, at a graduation party for 200 seniors at Forest Hills Central High School, the students voted to have no alcohol and no cars, so there would be no drinking and driving. In return, pleased parents donated funds to hire a rock group. The party was a big success.

While MADD, RID, and SADD are largely independent units, begun on a shoestring by individuals and small groups of citizens, they are gaining the recognition and support of some large and powerful national organizations. Among those heartily endorsing their efforts are the National Safety Council; the National Association of Governors Highway Safety Representatives; the American Insurance Association; the Government Employees Insurance Company; the Motor Vehicle Manufacturers Association; the American Automobile Association; the U.S. Brewer's Association; the Highway Users Federation; Citizens for Safe Drivers; the American Legion; the National Council on Alcoholism; the American Trauma Society; and the National Coalition for Emergency Medical Services, among others.

What effect is this new national effort having on the drunk-driving problem? How successful are MADD, RID, and other groups? Are they making even a dent in this huge, long-standing national problem? Consider the following:

■ Largely as a result of the efforts of citizen groups, beginning with New York in 1980, twenty-nine states have passed tougher drunk-driving laws. Iowa and five other states have passed the toughest laws in the nation to date. These center on deterrence and combining random checkpoints on highways with immediate suspension of a driver's license for ninety days. Washington, D.C., West Virginia, and Minnesota, along with Iowa, report a 45 to 51 percent drop in fatalities after these systems went into effect. And, largely as a result of the efforts of Candy Lightner and her colleagues in California, that state passed its own tougher drunk-driving law in 1982.

■ Shocked and angered when the drunk driver who killed their four-year-old daughter walked away from court with only a $284 fine and a suspended five-day jail sentence, despite a previous drunk-driving arrest, Mr. and Mrs. Mark Schuett of Ixonia, Wisconsin, took action. "This man got away with hitting and killing my child," said Mrs. Schuett. "Her life means more than a $284 fine." They took their case public and began a determined lobbying campaign. The resulting public support they gained, statewide, led to a new and tougher Wisconsin law that permits the state to suspend the license of anyone arrested for an alcohol-related driving offense, even before a trial.

■ Court monitoring by MADD and RID members and other relatives and friends of victims killed and injured in drunk-driving crashes has resulted in generally stiffer sentences being handed down to offenders by previously lenient judges.

[52]

But perhaps the single most dramatic evidence of the powerful influence of these citizen groups came in April 1982, when President Ronald Reagan, by executive order, created a national presidential commission on drunk driving. Such a blue ribbon panel had been sought for more than a year by Sandy Golden of Channel 9 News in Washington, D.C., Candy Lightner, and others.

When he announced the panel's formation on April 14, 1982, President Reagan said: "Americans are outraged that such slaughter of the innocent can take place on our highways. Our anger and frustration are matched only by the grief of those who have lost loved ones in such accidents. But there are useful, preventive measures we can take. The highway safety campaign that we are launching is aimed at the areas where a little prevention can pay big returns in saving lives and reducing injuries."

The president named John Volpe, former secretary of transportation, to head the commission. The executive order stated that the commission would undertake to:

(1) heighten public awareness of the seriousness of the drunk-driving problem;

(2) persuade states and communities to attack the drunk-driving problem in a more organized and systematic manner, including plans to eliminate bottlenecks in the arrest, trial, and sentencing processes that impair the effectiveness of many drunk-driving laws;

(3) encourage state and local officials and organizations to accept and use the latest techniques and methods to solve the problem; and

(4) generate public support for increased enforcement of state and local drunk-driving laws.

In signing the executive order, the president acknowledged the efforts of MADD, RID, SADD, and other groups and said: "The mood of the nation is ripe to make great headway against this problem, and that's exactly what we intend to do. By working together, we can look forward to creating greater safety on our streets and highways."

Commission Chairman Volpe said: "The basic problem is that it's so socially acceptable to drink and drive. I think we've got to bring public awareness up to the fact that drinking and driving is not socially acceptable."

Volpe also said he believed that the campaign against drunk drivers would be more successful today than past attempts have been. "Eleven years ago, when I was secretary of transportation, we spent $85 million on this problem, with only limited results. We didn't have the tremendous support of the media or the general public as we do now, and this can mean a big difference."

Other commission members include syndicated newspaper columnist Ann Landers; actor Dick Van Patten; Senator Robert Dole of Kansas; James S. Kemper, chairman of the Kemper Insurance Group; William N. Plymat, executive director of the American Council on Alcohol Problems; Vincent L. Tofany, president of the National Safety Council; and Candy Lightner.

Lightner said she hoped the commission would help by focusing attention on the issue. "Look what happened in the smoking situation," she said in an interview. "Smoking is no longer the big socially acceptable thing it used to be. People now criticize you for smoking. We need to do the same thing with drinking and driving."

There is mounting evidence that such an awareness is taking hold. In a recent survey conducted by the National Highway Traffic Safety Administration, 85 percent of respondents rated drunk driving as an "extremely important" or "very important" social problem; 41 percent of the people polled had "discussed the drunk-driving problem during the previous month"; and 57 percent said they could "recognize a potential drunk-driving situation."

"If our experience has taught us anything," Lightner says, "it is that we can make a difference if we choose to make that difference."

[54]

7
Getting Tougher

As nationwide public protest against drunk drivers continues to mount, it is having a profound effect on the laws of the land pertaining to this problem. State legislators, acknowledging the tidal waves of publicity generated by such groups as MADD and RID and bowing to their strong lobbying influence, are passing scores of tough new bills designed to crack down harder on drunk drivers. In 1981, nine states enacted such bills, and twenty-seven more states followed suit in 1982. Others are closely studying the situation.

The volumes of new legislation, from California to Massachusetts, could spell trouble with a capital "T" for violators, through stiffer sentences and more severe punishment. Many offenders are now being socked with mandatory jail sentences and heavy fines, even for a first arrest and conviction.

In California, for example, Governor Jerry Brown, on September 29, 1981, signed into law bill number AB541. It requires a minimum two-day jail sentence for a first offense of driving while intoxicated; a ten-day minimum jail sentence and fine, plus a one-year driver's license suspension for a second offense; and the possibility of a one-year jail sentence and $1,000 fine for any subsequent convictions.

[55]

At the same time, another new California law was signed, making it illegal to drive with a blood alcohol level of 0.10, while a third bill was passed increasing penalties for reckless driving involving alcohol use and restricting plea-bargaining to lesser charges in drunken-driving cases. A fourth bill authorized the hiring of 670 new California Highway Patrol officers to help enforce the new regulations. "It's time," Governor Brown said, "to put the drunk driver out of commission."

New York's state legislature in 1980 and 1981 passed several bills, providing restricted plea-bargaining for offenders, a minimum $350 fine, revocation of license for six months, and possible imprisonment for a first drunk-driving offense. For a second violation within ten years, the fine jumps to a minimum of $500. Previously, each convicted drunk driver in the state had paid an average fine of only $12.

Virginia legislators, influenced by the strong lobbying campaign by state MADD members, passed tougher laws in July 1982. Under them, first offenders, upon conviction, lose their driver's licenses for six months, can be fined up to $1,000, and can be sentenced to up to twelve months in jail. Second offenders convicted within five years of the first charge will be automatically jailed for forty-eight hours, lose their license to drive for up to three years, and can be fined up to $1,000. They may also receive longer jail sentences at the discretion of the courts.

In Massachusetts, on September 1, 1982, lawmakers decreed that first offenders will pay fines of between $100 and $1,000 and will lose their licenses for one year. They can also spend up to two years in jail or be forced to pay $400 for participation in an alcohol-education program. Persons convicted of drunken driving three times or more will receive mandatory prison terms, and drunken drivers convicted of killing another person will receive a mandatory one-year jail sentence. Said Governor

[56]

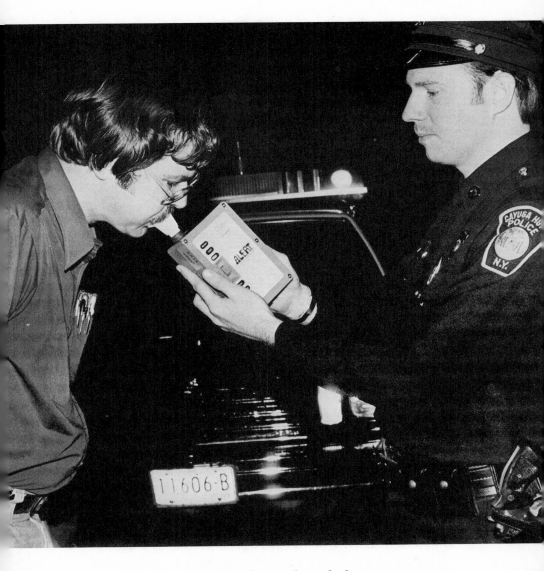

*A motorist submits to a breathalyzer exam
administered by a law enforcement officer.
Breathalyzer tests are used extensively by
police to combat the drunk-driver problem.*

Edward J. King upon signing the bill: "Let the word go out now, to anyone who might consider driving under the influence, that drunk driving will no longer be tolerated."

Maine also passed a new law in September 1982. Under it, first-time offenders found guilty of drunken driving face mandatory license suspension, a fine, or a minimum of two days in jail, with stiffer penalties for repeat offenders. In Michigan, a new law allows police to detain drivers whom they suspect of drinking. Previously, an officer had to either see an accident or find a witness to it. Consequently, arrests of drunk drivers in that state have increased by 21 percent.

Under a new Arizona law, those convicted of driving while intoxicated are slapped into jail for a minimum one-day sentence. If violators refuse to submit to a blood-alcohol–level test, their licenses are automatically revoked for six months. They may also be required to obtain treatment under court supervision. Second and subsequent convictions within a two-year period result in a minimum sixty-day jail sentence.

One of the most severe penalties of all awaits repeat violators in the state of Louisiana. There, first-time drunk drivers face a sixty-day license suspension, a fine of $100 to $400, and the possibility of imprisonment for a period of thirty days to six months. Those convicted a second time will be imprisoned for from 125 days to six months, and third-time losers will be locked up for from one to five years. A fourth conviction carries a sentence of from ten to thirty years in prison at hard labor.

Many judges across the nation are using the new laws to pound home the point that drunk driving is a serious offense. In Denver, for example, in 1982, County Judge Irving Ettenberg sentenced a sixteen-year-old girl to six months in the state women's prison for an alcohol-related driving conviction. Two weeks earlier, she had been before the same judge and pleaded guilty to a drunk-driving charge.

[58]

Another case, which was tried in rural Fauquier County, Virginia, in September 1982, may have set a precedent that should strike fear into the heart of anyone who drives and drinks. A court jury there found a twenty-five-year-old man guilty of three counts of second-degree murder for an auto accident he had caused while driving intoxicated. Three people, including two teenage girls, had been killed in the accident. The jury recommended he be sentenced to five years in prison on each of the three counts.

The case made national headlines because it is so rare that a murder conviction is handed down for drunk driving. Here's what happened: On the night of November 20, 1981, witnesses testified that they saw Warren W. Essex's car swerve in and out of its lane, pass other vehicles on hills, and run through a red light. Minutes later, Essex's car crossed the center line of State Route 28 and collided head-on with a pickup truck carrying three teenagers. Two of the teens, and a passenger in Essex's vehicle, were killed. Three hours after the crash, a blood sample showed Essex' blood-alcohol level still well in excess of 0.10.

In presenting their case, prosecutors argued that Essex, by driving while drunk and operating his car recklessly, turned the vehicle into a "deadly weapon." In Virginia, the law defines a deadly weapon as an object "that is likely to cause death or great bodily injury because of the manner, and under the circumstances, in which it is used." At the trial, Assistant Commonwealth Attorney Roger A. Inger said: "Take a man and put him in that automobile, that 3,600-pound [1,600-kg] mass of steel, and put him behind the wheel when he's intoxicated, and you've got a man with a loaded gun. . . . Mr. Essex committed an act, the consequences of which were foreseeable, or should have been, by an ordinary man. To do that act anyway is evidence of a callous disregard for the life of others. . . . It has always been against the law to kill people."

[59]

In December 1981, the California Supreme Court struck down the statute that all vehicular homicides in the state must be tried as manslaughter. It ruled that "a drunken driver can face murder charges if he is involved in a fatal car crash." In so doing, the high court reinstated two second-degree murder charges against Robert Lee Watson, saying he "exhibited wantonness and conscious disregard for human life."

Watson was allegedly going 84 miles (135 km) per hour in a 35 mph (56 kmph) zone when he struck two cars and killed two people, one a young girl. His blood-alcohol content was .23 percent, more than twice the legal limit. In the subsequent trial, Shasta County Superior Court granted Watson's motion to dismiss the murder counts on grounds that the acts did not demonstrate malice.

However, the state appealed, and the Supreme Court later said the facts supported a finding of implied malice, which justified a murder charge. Malice may be implied, the court ruled, "when a defendant does an act with a high probability that it will result in death and does it with a base antisocial motive and with a wanton disregard for human life."

Although many of the new state laws have been on the books for only a few months or a year or two, there is already impressive evidence that stepped up enforcement of the laws plus the threat of tougher penalties are proving to be effective deterrents. For example, in Maine, where mandatory jail sentences for first-time offenders are now law, there has been a 47 percent reduction in alcohol-related fatalities.

In July and August 1982, the first two months after a stiff new state law was enacted in Florida, arrests of drunk drivers were up 70 percent over the corresponding period of the previous year. More troopers were assigned to work weekends and later hours, when drunk driving is more prevalent. State authorities credited the crackdown with being largely responsible for a 10 percent decline in Florida traffic fatalities through the first eight months of 1982. Those convicted under the new law must do fifty hours of community-service work, pay a fine of at least $250, and surrender their licenses for up to six months for the first offense.

But perhaps nowhere is there a more dramatic case for the positive effect of tough laws and a strong anti–drunk-driving media campaign than in the state of Oregon. Here, the crackdown began in 1971. Oregon pioneered the concept that being caught driving with a blood-alcohol level of .10 or above was not just evidence of intoxication but a crime in itself. Also, certain offenses carry mandatory jail sentences, and drunk-driving incidents stay on a driver's record. Further, the state inaugurated the concept of having citizens report drunk drivers they see on the road.

The results? In the period from 1971 through 1981, despite a 46 percent increase in drivers and a 62 percent hike in the number of vehicles on the road, the rate in Oregon traffic fatalities has plunged 35 percent.

A growing number of national organizations are voicing their support of the new laws. One is the National Association of Independent Insurers, a trade association of over 500 insurance companies that underwrite approximately 40 percent of all automobile casualty insurance in the United States. Says the NAII: "We are supporting the concepts of suspending drivers' licenses through automatic administrative sanctions rather than court procedures; using random spot road checks to apprehend more drunk-driving violators; tightening rules for administering tests for intoxication; and issuing community-service sentences and/or work-release sentencing utilizing special jail facilities [such as closed school buildings], particularly for first-time offenders."

But, as impressive as the early statistics are regarding a decline in drunk-driving incidents following passage of stiffer laws and an enforcement crackdown, not everyone agrees that this is the best answer to the problem.

After the passage of the new California laws, for instance, thirty-eight counties sued the state, claiming they didn't have the money to enforce the laws. In Colorado, opponents of proposed new legislation involving more mandatory jail sentences for drunk drivers argued that even if there was enough money to carry out the program, there wasn't enough jail space. Indeed, some authorities have warned that strict enforcement of new laws across the nation could result in hundreds of thousands of arrests annually. If mandatory jail sentences were applied, where, these experts ask, would all these offenders be put?

"The approach to increase the severity of punishment and to encourage people to stop drinking won't work," declares Dr. Joseph Gusfield, a sociologist with the University of California at San Diego. "In San Diego County alone, we have 26,000 drunk-driving arrests each year; and judges just aren't going to fill up the jails with these people."

Gusfield and other sociologists are convinced that harsh jail penalties only result in police officers' giving reduced charges at the time of arrests, and in judges and juries becoming more reluctant to convict because they consider the penalties unduly severe. Rather, these experts recommend automatic license revocations and permanent recording of drunk-driving arrests on driving records.

Adds the National Council on Alcoholism: "We are concerned that the adoption of mandatory sentencing may give rise to plea-bargaining resulting in the substitution of charges that are not alcohol-related [such as reckless driving], thereby possibly inhibiting the detection and treatment of the alcoholic and the problem drinker. Any legislation that imposes penalties for drunk driving should also include provisions for alcoholism treatment."

Still another argument against the effectiveness of tougher laws, especially over the long term, is raised by the Insurance Institute for Highway Safety. This organization cites results found in a comprehensive study done some time ago entitled "Deterrence of the Drinking Driver: An International Survey," conducted by H. Laurence Ross and sponsored by the National Highway Traffic Safety Administration.

Ross researched scientific literature on the effectiveness of drinking/driving laws in more than twelve countries. "Evidence was found," he said, "that adoption and enforcement of these laws nearly always has had a deterrent effect," resulting in reductions in serious casualties during the main drinking hours. Unfortunately, Ross added, these deterrent effects were consistently found to be of only temporary duration. "Crashes and casualties approached prior trends within a few months, or, at most, a few years of the reform."

The report said that drivers appear initially to believe that the law will be effectively enforced, and during this time there is a deterrent effect on alcohol-impaired driving. However, as time goes on, and drivers accurately perceive that the risk of apprehension is in fact low, the deterrent effect is reduced, and, ultimately, lost altogether.

Ross backed his conclusion with statistics based on a number of other studies. He said that a driver would have to commit from 200 to 2,000 driving-while-intoxicated violations to be caught. And, after the apprehension, there still would be only a fifty-fifty chance of the driver's experiencing anything more than a mild punishment such as a small fine.

To mount and maintain an effective long-term anti-drunk-driving program, the study suggested, in addition to the certainty, severity, and swiftness of the punishment decreed by new and tougher laws, the public's perception of the likelihood of being apprehended has to be considered and dealt with. Says the Insurance Institute

[63]

for Highway Safety: "If alcohol-impaired drivers do not perceive that they are likely to be apprehended for their offenses, then even the threat of certain punishment if caught will not stop them from driving or stop the tragedy of human suffering from crashes they cause."

Thus, the debate over whether or not harsher penalties, such as mandatory jail sentences, can permanently reduce the drunk-driving problem will likely continue for some time to come, especially since so many states have only recently passed new laws. Still, a recent national Gallup poll determined that 77 percent of all Americans support mandatory prison sentences, even for first-time offenders. And whatever you believe, it is difficult to argue with the point made by Senator Curtis Person of Tennessee, who sponsored that state's stricter bills while realizing the court and prison overcrowding problem they might cause. "I was more concerned," he said, "about the overcrowding of hospitals, morgues, and cemeteries."

8
Raising the Drinking Age

The year 1971 was an eventful one for America's teenagers. That was the year when ratification of the Twenty-sixth Amendment to the Constitution of the United States gave the right to vote to anyone eighteen years old or older. Previously, one had to be twenty-one to exercise this privilege.

In a way, the Vietnam War helped bring this amendment about. The argument and rationale was that if teenagers could risk their lives fighting for their country halfway around the world in Indochina, how could their government deny them the right to vote?

Following the general mood of the times, twenty-six states in the early 1970s lowered the age at which young people could drink legally, from twenty-one to eighteen in most cases. Again, the reasoning was that if teenagers were old enough to wage war and to vote, then they were old enough to drink.

Such an argument was, naturally, endorsed by teenagers. But many sociologists, psychologists, law-enforcement officers, juvenile authorities, and other experts had sincere doubts about these new laws. These opponents of a lowered drinking age believed the following results might happen:

■ The younger the person is, the less likely it is that he or she will drink alcohol moderately and responsibly.

■ More youngsters would begin to drink at an earlier age (especially among thirteen- to seventeen-year-olds).

■ Those who already drink would drink more.

■ There would be an increase in alcohol-related problems, such as drunk driving, motor vehicle collisions, public drunkenness, lowered school attendance, and alcoholism.

But others argued in favor of the lowered drinking age. They pointed out:

■ The use of alcohol was already widespread among youth between the ages of eighteen and twenty-one and even among those younger than eighteen; therefore, any law prohibiting alcohol would be difficult to enforce, or would be selectively or unfairly enforced.

■ A law difficult to enforce, or which is unfairly administered, would turn off many young people to laws in general, producing a "hell-with-it" attitude.

■ The use of alcohol was already widespread among those younger than eighteen, and a lowering of the drinking age would not have a significant effect on alcohol consumption by the younger population.

■ It would be inconsistent to lower the age of majority for such acts as voting and the ability to enter into a binding contract and, at the same time, forbid the purchase and consumption of alcohol or employment in places where alcohol is served.

It did not take long to realize that the opponents of lowering the legal drinking age were chillingly accurate in at least one of their forecasts—that there would be a sharp rise in alcohol-related motor vehicle accidents among teenagers. Stark statistics soon backed their assumptions.

Iowa, for example, lowered its legal drinking age from twenty-one to eighteen in 1973. There was an immediate increase in the number of youths killed as a result of driving while drinking. In the four years from 1970 to 1974, 124 teenagers died in such accidents. In the four years from 1974 to 1978, the number rose to 194.

Connecticut lowered the legal drinking age from twenty to eighteen in 1972. Three years later, the percentage of drinking teenagers involved in all of the state's accidents had jumped from 13 to 24 percent. And during that same time, the number of teenagers arrested for drunk driving increased 50 percent.

Illinois dropped the legal drinking age from twenty-one to nineteen in 1973. By 1977, the number of traffic accidents involving teenagers and alcohol had risen 33 percent. Arizona lowered its drinking age from twenty-one to nineteen in 1971, and within four years the number of drinking teenagers involved in traffic fatalities nearly doubled.

In perhaps no other state were the statistics as alarming as in New Jersey. Here, the average number of persons killed annually by eighteen to twenty-year-old drivers climbed by 176 percent after the state lowered its drinking age to eighteen. Commented New Jersey State Senator C. Louis Bassano: "Statistics have shown us that kids can't handle alcohol. It's an experiment that has failed."

Says the Insurance Institute for Highway Safety: "In a study of various states and Canadian provinces that reduced their drinking ages from twenty-one to eighteen, there were significant increases in fatal crash involvement—particularly in nighttime and single vehicle crashes in which alcohol is most often involved—of drivers under twenty-one in these areas, compared with adjacent areas that did not reduce their drinking ages. These increases occurred not only among eighteen- to twenty-year-olds, who were directly affected by the law change, but also among fifteen- to seventeen-year-olds."

According to a Department of Transportation national survey, there has been an overall increase of 28 percent in the number of alcohol-related traffic accidents involving the "under twenty" driver since the early 1970s, when more than half the states lowered the legal drinking age. Such findings caused the Transportation Department and the National Highway Traffic Safety Administration to "unanimously attribute the steadily worsening under-twenty driving record to the national trend toward lower legal drinking ages."

Shocked at the closely drawn parallel between the lowered legal drinking age and the corresponding steep rise in alcohol-related accidents among young people, many of the states have since rewritten their laws, raising the legal drinking age back up to twenty-one. Others have such legislation pending.

These laws began taking force in the mid- to late 1970s, and, again, the statistical story is amazing. In Minnesota, which raised the legal drinking age from eighteen to nineteen in 1976, there was a healthy 56 percent decrease in the deaths of young drivers in the three years immediately following the new law. In Michigan, alcohol-related teenage vehicle crashes dropped 31 percent in one year after the legal drinking age was raised from eighteen to twenty-one in 1978. New Hampshire reported a 75 percent decline in traffic deaths among young persons after it boosted its drinking age from eighteen back to twenty in 1979.

In 1981 a research report entitled "The Effect of Raising the Legal Minimum Drinking Age on Fatal Crash Involvement," conducted by Dr. Paul L. Zador, a behaviorial scientist, and members of the Insurance Institute for Highway Safety was published. In this report, nine

states that had raised their legal drinking age were closely studied. The new laws, the study disclosed, "resulted
in reductions in fatal crash involvement among drivers
the law changes applied to, especially in types of fatal
crashes in which alcohol is most often involved. The
reductions in the nighttime fatal crash involvement of
such drivers, that occurred in eight of the nine states,
ranged from 6 to 75 percent. On average, a state that
raises its drinking age can expect about a 28 percent
reduction in nighttime fatal crash involvement among
drivers the law change applies to."

Further, the report said: "It was estimated that in
fourteen [other] states that had raised their drinking
ages as of January 1981, the result is about 380 fewer
young drivers involved in nighttime fatal crashes. In the
thirty-one states that still had a legal minimum drinking
age less than twenty-one [as of January 1981], it is estimated that each year there could be about 730 fewer
young drivers in nighttime fatal crashes if the legal
drinking age was raised to twenty-one."

The report concluded: "The societal benefits achieved
in states that have raised their drinking ages are substantial; the benefits achieved by additional states raising
their drinking ages would be even more substantial.
Raising the legal minimum drinking age to twenty-one in
all states would have an important impact in reducing
the annual toll of motor vehicle deaths in the United
States, particularly the deaths of young people and of
others with whom they are involved in crashes."

Many experts say that the Insurance Institute for
Highway Safety study and other studies affirm that a
legal minimum drinking age of twenty-one is an effective
countermeasure against alcohol-related accidents by
young drivers. Cites a report in the *Journal of American
Insurance*: "The ease with which alcoholic beverages can
be obtained—and its visibility in the social environ-
ment—affect the amount and pattern of alcohol con-

sumption and therefore the incidence of alcohol-related health problems. With a higher legal drinking age, young persons have more difficulty getting alcohol, so they have less, consume less, do less driving under its influence, and are therefore involved in fewer alcohol-related motor vehicle accidents."

Some authorities, however, contend that the emphasis being given to raising legal drinking ages in an effort to lower teenage traffic accidents is being overplayed. Other research reports, for instance, have indicated that there already was a major rise in such accidents before many states lowered their legal drinking-age laws. Said one such study: "The change in the law may be more reflective of an already occurring change in drinking behavior, rather than a subsequent change."

Other experts argue that raising minimum drinking ages tends to encourage eighteen- to twenty-year-olds to drink in unmonitored situations, such as parties or on the highways, rather than in more controlled atmospheres. Still others say that raising the drinking age punishes eighteen-year-olds without dealing directly with the drunk-driving problem, which led investigators and the public to reconsider the lowered ages in the first place. These critics believe that the evidence showing a correlation between lowered drinking ages and higher rates of alcohol-related accidents is not conclusive. They point to studies in some states that showed an increase in arrests for drunk driving even after the minimum age was raised.

Another criticism voiced is that legal age requirements do not prevent teenagers from getting alcohol, particularly since many get it at home. "It's pretty well established that laws in and of themselves do not change social customs," says Dr. Geraldo Gonzales of the University of Florida. Supporters of this view agree that changing laws will not change the causes of teenage drinking, which are symptomatic of a larger societal problem with alcohol consumption.

[70]

Still, a large majority of authorities believe that the raising of drinking-age laws does have a positive effect on the teenage drunk-driving problem. Summing up the feelings of many, a national group called Medicine in the Public Interest said that "even though a minimum-age law frequently may be violated, it may help prevent drinking among some young teenagers."

Supporting this contention are the findings from a national survey among college students. Some 36 percent of those from states where the minimum drinking age was twenty-one said they would have drunk more had there been no age restrictions on drinking.

Declares Charles Yoakum, an insurance official, "Statistics clearly show that too often the teenage drinker drives, and because of his inexperience with both drinking and driving, he becomes involved in a disproportionate number of accidents. To protect him—as well as the thousands of innocent motorists and pedestrians who also are killed and injured in these accidents—we must move to raise the legal drinking age again. The teenage driver has not proved that he can handle the responsibility. And the price of failure is too high."

9
A National Law

"Drunk driving is a national epidemic that threatens every American in every congressional district across the nation," says U.S. Congressman Michael D. Barnes of Maryland. "Drunk driving is the most frequently committed violent crime in the United States today."

Barnes is a pioneer among a swelling number of members of the U.S. House of Representatives and Senate, who are pushing hard for new national legislation aimed at reducing the annual toll taken by alcohol-related accidents. Barnes and his colleagues believe that the federal government can play an important part in the war against drunk driving.

To this end, Barnes and Congressman James J. Howard of New Jersey sponsored a new bill—H.R. 6170—that will, through the use of incentive grants, reward states that adopt comprehensive, coordinated, community-based drunk-driver control programs. Barnes explains that this will not cost the American taxpayer an extra cent. The money, he says, will come from existing revenues in the Highway Trust Fund.

The Howard-Barnes bill will make $25 million available to states in the first year after its enactment and $50 million in each of the next two years. "These funds,"

Barnes says, "will be used as 'seed money' to assist and reward those states taking effective steps toward establishing comprehensive, ultimately self-sufficient, programs aimed at deterring drunk driving and assuring swift and sure arrest, conviction, punishment, and rehabilitation of the offender."

In essence, H.R. 6170 recommends that states consider adopting certain standards, including:

(1) enhanced enforcement supported by an increased public awareness of the problem.

(2) a statewide record system tracking repeat offenders, one that is easily accessible to the courts and public.

(3) establishing a blood-alcohol concentration level of .10 percent to be deemed as driving while intoxicated. (Most, but not all, states have this in force today.)

(4) presentence screening of offenders for sanctioning purposes.

(5) automatic suspension or revocation of an offender's driving license.

(6) providing the courts with the following sanction options for all persons convicted of driving while intoxicated: community service, fines, and imprisonment, in addition to attendance in either alcohol-safety education or alcohol treatment programs.

The bill provides that the secretary of transportation sponsor public hearings to allow comment on the possible elements of an effective, comprehensive, and coordinated program. The secretary would then establish the specific criteria with which to judge how the states are performing and how much federal assistance the states should receive from the incentive grant program.

In the U.S. Senate, Claiborne Pell of Rhode Island has for years led a drive to have a tough national drunk-driving law passed by Congress. Senator Pell has a strong personal interest; two of his staff members have been killed by drunk drivers. "Local law enforcement is

In this exhibit at the Museum of the City of New York, some possible consequences of drunk driving are shown. Note especially the crushed tricycle alongside the damaged left tire.

clearly the first line of defense against drunk drivers," he says. "Our job as federal legislators is to provide the tools that will enable local law-enforcement officials to keep these potential killers off our highways."

Like the Barnes bill in the House, Pell's legislation would draw upon existing federal funds to give grants to states as incentives to enact and enforce the law. Title I of the bill would establish an incentive grant program for the states that enact a comprehensive drunk-driver statute. States that adopt the bill's provisions, which include automatic license suspension, mandatory jail sentences for repeat offenders, alcohol treatment programs, and improved enforcement of drunk-driver laws, will automatically qualify for additional highway-safety funding to carry out the program.

The bill favors strong punishment. It calls for the adoption of statutes that would:

■ require "prompt suspension" of licenses of persons caught while intoxicated—ninety days for a first offender and one year for repeat offenders.

■ impose a ninety-day impoundment of the vehicle of anyone caught driving during a period when his or her license has been suspended for drunk driving.

■ jail any person convicted of driving while intoxicated more than once in a five-year period for a minimum of forty-eight hours, with no suspensions of sentences or probations allowed.

As with the Barnes bill in the House, the Senate bill, as a basic provision, calls for the state's acceptance of a .10 blood alcohol content test result as proof of intoxication. The Pell bill's requirement of alcohol-treatment programs suggests that states use presentence screening and assessment to identify individuals who are problem drinkers or who suffer from the disease of alcoholism, and to refer them to local treatment programs and facilities. It also recommends that states seriously consider the inclusion of alcohol-abuse prevention and alcohol-education information in driver-education programs. Another element of the bill requires states to set up driver record systems that identify repeat offenders and make such data readily accessible to the state courts.

Under Title I of the bill, $75 million would be authorized out of the existing Highway Trust Fund—$25 million for the first year and $50 million for the second. "The additional funding authorized by this bill is insignificant compared to the loss of life, family tragedy, and health impairment we presently live with and pay for as a society," says Senator Pell. "Legislation alone, of course, is not the whole answer. Drunk driving will never disappear entirely, until public attitudes and outrage demand an end to it. What this bill will do is strongly reinforce efforts already under way in most states to increase the penalties for drunk drivers and—most critically—get them off our highways through a combination of better law enforcement and automatic license suspension.

"There is not a single country in the world that has a higher rate of alcohol-related traffic fatalities than the United States," Senator Pell says. "After thirty-five years of slogans reminding drinkers not to drive, we need to impose stiffer penalties for drunk driving if we hope to reduce the annual carnage on our highways.

"A car with an intoxicated driver is precisely as dangerous as a loaded gun in the hands of someone blinded by rage—the combination of an instrument with the power to kill and a person who is past the powers of reason is precisely the same in both cases. Drunk driving has flourished in the United States primarily because we have tolerated it."

Critics of the legislation proposed in the Howard-Barnes and Pell bills contend that the drunk-driving problem should be policed and handled by the states, not the federal government. In fact, Arizona Governor Bruce Babbitt called for the president to veto such bills unless they were suitably amended to give more control to the states.

"The crusade against drunk driving is worthy and popular," Governor Babbitt says. "But popular causes have a history of expanding the reach of the federal government. That expansion erodes the vitality of the states and establishes a relationship of intergovernmental welfare dependency. For all its horrors, drunk driving is no more a federal issue than are murder, housebreaking, jaywalking, and hundreds of other crimes traditionally handled by state and local authorities.

"The congressmen rushing to enact a federal drunk-driving law ought to tell us whether they would also advocate federal laws governing use of the death penalty, punishing housebreakers, specifying a national minimum drinking age, or mandating penalties for child abuse. If not, how do they distinguish such issues from drunk driving?"

Proponents of the bills counter such arguments. Says U.S. Senator John C. Danforth of Missouri: "Of course, the federal government should not be responsible for policing the highways. But it is uniquely able to foster wider acceptance of effective anti–drunk-driving measures among the states. The Senate bill takes the long-overdue step of presenting meritorious efforts in one state as examples to other states that have not yet come to grips with the problem."

Senator Danforth adds that the federal government has an "enormous financial stake" in reducing highway deaths and injuries. "Drunk driving costs society up to $17 billion every year. The National Highway Traffic Safety Administration has estimated that as much as $3.8 billion falls directly on the shoulders of the taxpayer through lost tax revenues, Social Security, and disability payments to people who are injured or the families of those who are killed in automobile accidents.

[78]

"The legislative history of the Highway Safety Act of 1966 and the National Traffic and Motor Vehicle Safety Act of 1966 clearly shows Congress's legitimate concern over the direct financial interest of the federal government in highway safety. Under these two acts, the federal government sets motor vehicle safety standards, investigates safety defects, and hands out $80 million in highway-safety grants directly to the states every year. The federal role in promoting safety on the highways is as well established as participation in building highways in the first place."

The Howard-Barnes and Pell bills have received enthusiastic support from MADD, RID, the National Association of Governors' Highway Safety Representatives, the Motor Vehicle Manufacturers Association, the Highway Users Federation, the American Automobile Association, the American Insurance Association, the Government Employees Insurance Company, the National Council on Alcoholism, Citizens for Safe Drivers, and various other groups. Typical of this support is that voiced by Dr. William E. Corgill, secretary of the National Association of Governors' Highway Safety Representatives, in a congressional hearing on drunk-driving legislation in April 1982: "While the epidemic caused by drunk drivers is national in scope, we are convinced that the problem can be most effectively dealt with at the state and local levels," says Dr. Corgill. "This legislation [the Howard-Barnes bill] will go a long way toward supporting state and local efforts attacking the problem by recommending comprehensive programs, providing incentives, and spurring immediate actions."

Proponents also point to specific cases where the infusion of federal funds is having a direct impact on helping states attack the drunk-driving problem. In Maryland, for instance, the arrest rate of intoxicated drivers rose 109 percent following a federal grant of $150,000, which paid state troopers to work overtime, particularly on weekends, to catch drunk motorists.

[79]

Congressman Barnes points out that Montgomery County, Maryland, is one of the first communities in the nation to set up roadblocks, or "sobriety checkpoints," aimed at nabbing those who drive and drink. Says Barnes: "I had the opportunity to join Captain John Baker one Saturday night at a roadblock, and I found the public support among drivers stopped to be nearly unanimous."

This is just the type of program, Barnes added, that can be supported by incentive funds granted by the federal government. He also cites a Maryland program inaugurated by community, business, and government leaders called "Projection Graduation," designed to encourage high school students to find alternatives to driving while under the influence of alcohol, particularly during the traditionally dangerous prom season.

"I point to these various initiatives," the congressman says, "to emphasize the kinds of creative efforts the Howard-Barnes bill can help to inspire potentially in every community nationwide."

In October 1982, the Howard-Barnes bill was signed into law; the Pell bill was still pending in Congress but is expected to pass in the near future. Such laws, say backers of the bills, represent a major battle won in the continuing war against drunk driving.

At "sobriety checkpoints,"
motorists suspected of
being drunk can quickly
be tested by a device
such as this.

10
What Can Happen – To You

You're a teenager who has just been stopped by the
police at 11:30 p.m. on a Friday night, after you were
observed running a red light and recklessly changing
lanes in heavy traffic. You've had too much to drink, and
you know it. The law officers confirm this on the spot by
giving you a blood-alcohol level breath analyzer test.
You register .13, well in excess of the .10 which, by law,
determines you are driving while under the influence of
alcohol. Now you wish you had listened to your friends
and let someone drive you home, but it's too late.

You are in trouble, but how much trouble? You have
no previous driving citations. Will the police slap cuffs on
you, fingerprint you, throw you in a jail cell with hard-
ened criminals, and toss away the key? Should you call a
lawyer? You've heard about the tougher drunk-driving
laws in your state, but you never thought you'd get
caught. You didn't kill or maim anyone or cause an accident, so that should be in your favor. Still, you are
scared.

What can you realistically expect to happen to you? It
is a question all who drive and drink should ask themselves. While the punishment for drunk driving varies in
individual states, and is dependent upon the seriousness

of the offense and subject to the discretion of the judge to be faced, the following scenario may be close to what you would actually experience under the circumstances described above.

Most states have some form of Alcohol Safety Action Program, ASAP for short. The chances are likely, since this was your first violation and did not involve an accident, that you will assigned to such a program. Let's assume this is the case. The judge trying your case will probably offer you an "opportunity" for voluntary participation in an ASAP program. The details of the program will be explained to you later.

You can choose to enroll in such a program, or you can turn it down. It is not too smart to do the latter. The case against you is ironclad. You were caught driving while under the influence, tried before the judge, and found guilty. If you do not enter the ASAP program, you will probably receive a punishment much more severe—a healthy fine, for example, and a strong likelihood of spending time either in jail or in community service.

You choose to enroll. Now what happens? First, the judge assigns a date for you to report to your local ASAP office. You must pay a fee to participate in this program. For sake of example, let's say you are in Virginia. There, the fee is $200.

You report to the ASAP officer on the assigned date. You meet with, say, twenty others, who, like you, have been convicted of driving while under the influence of alcohol. They are of both sexes and all ages, from sixteen to seventy, all races and colors, and from all walks of life. You are embarrassed, but there is some relief in knowing that everyone there is in the same boat as you.

You participate in a group session, and then you are individually interviewed by an ASAP officer. This is the classification portion of the program. From this, it is determined which level of the program you will be admitted to. In Virginia, there are three: Level I is for light, occasional, or social drinkers; Level II is for those either considered problem drinkers or whose patterns of drinking behavior may be leading them to become problem drinkers; and Level III, basically, is for alcoholics.

It is determined, from previous examination of records and from the interview, that you should be assigned to the Level I program. The programs for Levels II and III last much longer and are more complex because the participants in them have deeper drinking problems than you.

It is explained at the outset that you will be required to attend a sixteen-hour driver-education course over the next four weeks, and you must attend *every* session. If you miss even one for any reason other than severe illness or something comparable, you will be "washed out" of the program, and you will have to go back before the judge. You will probably be fined, have your driver's license taken away, and may face a jail sentence. Plus, you will forfeit the $200 ASAP entrance fee.

So, over the next few weeks, you learn a lot about alcohol and its effects on your body, especially those related to driving. You learn all about driving. You are taught how to improve your skills, and you increase your knowledge of driving rules and laws. You learn how to improve your attitude while driving, as well as your sense of responsibility.

But perhaps more important, you learn a lot about yourself. Through the films, books, lectures, and group discussions, you gain valuable insight on how to examine and evaluate your own drinking habits. You find out how to identify "alternative life-style patterns," which may include only limited social drinking or, possibly, total abstinence from all alcoholic beverages. And, you learn to develop a positive attitude concerning the use and/or abuse of alcohol, especially while driving a motor vehicle.

In all, it is an impressive program, and it makes a solid

impact on you. You are shocked to see the devastating results of filmed accidents caused by irresponsible drunk drivers. You are jarred at the visions of mangled, crippled lives, ruined in a split second. You are sobered by the testimony of law officers who deal with drunk drivers daily. You are scared at finding out what can happen to you if you continue driving and drinking. You are alarmed at what will happen to you if, after completing the program, you are caught and convicted again of driving while under the influence.

You say you have learned your lesson. When you have successfully completed the program, you go back before the judge for final sentencing. The fact that you took the ASAP course is in your favor, and your sentence is suspended. You have been through a wringing experience, one that has proved valuable, but one which you do not wish to go through again, ever.

National statistics indicate that very few persons who go through such an alcohol-safety action program are caught and convicted a second time for driving while under the influence. Generally, the figure is somewhere between 5 and 10 percent.

"We see very few social drinkers as repeat offenders," says Theodore L. Fitzgerald, director of the Peninsula ASAP program in Newport News, Virginia. "With most of these people, it is like touching a hot stove. A rational person won't do it again."

Adds one teenage Newport News ASAP graduate: "I never thought I would think like this, but $200 is a small price for what I learned in this course. I haven't had anything to drink since I took this course and have no intentions of drinking again. I just wish more people would see the problems drinking can cause before it becomes critical."

Though some critics have charged that ASAP programs amount to only a "slap on the wrist" and enable many to soon be back on the road again, driving and drinking, it is generally conceded that such programs are effective with most people who are exposed to them. But there is still a problem with the system. "We have a significant impact on the drunk driver we catch," says Fitzgerald. "But then statistics say we catch only one drunk driver for every 500 or 1,000, or even 2,000, others who are on the road. They're the ones who believe that getting caught is something that happens to other people, not them."

To help tackle this, many states have added public information campaigns to their ASAP programs. Experts visit schools, church groups, and other organizations, spreading the message of the dangers of mixing alcohol and driving. "We believe this has a definite positive effect," says Fitzgerald, "but we have a long way to go. When a sufficient number of people recognize drunk driving as the serious problem it is, then we'll get somewhere. I think we're heading in the right direction. Public awareness is improving. I'm encouraged.

"Meanwhile, we'll continue working with drunk drivers, the public, police, and the courts to reduce alcohol-related crashes, injuries, and fatalities, through ASAP education and alcohol-treatment programs. We may be reaching only a small percentage of those who need to receive the message, but every person we convince to stay off the road after they've been drinking is a step forward."

11 Answers to the Problem

"Education is by far the most potent weapon available in the struggle against drunk driving," says the National Highway Traffic Safety Administration. "We can't make much headway in changing the way people act until we change the way they think . . . and until we help our society develop more responsible social standards governing the use of alcohol, particularly where driving is involved."

Adds Dr. William E. Corgill, secretary of the National Association of Governors' Highway Safety Representatives: "Noteworthy success will only be achieved when alcohol abuse is universally accepted as a major public health problem in this country."

Most experts and authorities agree that the greatest potential for helping curb the drunk-driving problem lies in alcohol education, especially the education of preteenage students. "Educators tell us that attitudes toward drinking are formulated at a young age and that they are fairly well in place by the time a youngster becomes a teenager," says Dr. Corgill. "This illustrates the need for primary prevention and education programs at the elementary school level."

Some researchers, in fact, advocate introduction of

[89]

alcohol education as early as the first grade. "Even children at six and seven years of age have some very clear notions about alcohol and its effects," says Dr. Gerald Globetti, a University of Alabama sociologist.

The National Highway Traffic Safety Administration calls the influence of teachers in developing alcohol-related values among young people "second only to the parents themselves." Teachers, the NHTSA points out, "control a captive audience of impressionable young minds, an audience that is more receptive to new ideas and new ways of thinking and acting than any other group in our society. Not only does this provide an exceptional opportunity for structuring mature attitudes toward drinking and driving, but it places teachers in a position of greater responsibility—particularly when you consider the fact that half of all boys and girls in the fourteen to eighteen age group report being in alcohol-related situations once a month or more."

The NHTSA concludes: "Never has the need for effective alcohol/driving education programs been greater than it is right now. And no one in our society is in a better position to implement and support such programs than teachers are."

Some organizations call for an educational program, beginning at the earliest possible age, that would stress the appropriate and inappropriate uses of alcohol. One suggested approach says teachers should not make any moral judgments and should point out that alcohol has many appropriate uses in our culture. Inappropriate uses, such as in situations where one is driving, should be discussed as being excessively dangerous. Stress should be placed on where, when, and how to use alcohol.

According to the Distilled Spirits Council of the United States (DISCUS), "Most adolescents, and most adults as well, are very poorly informed about alcohol. Those discussing beverage alcohol frequently repeat, and believe, statements which have no basis in fact. Myth, folklore, and misinterpretation of statistical data have taken the place of accuracy in common parlance."

Although some form of alcohol education is required in every state, DISCUS believes that much of the material taught is outdated and counterproductive and that educational methods in the field "are tangled in confusion. When, to whom, by whom, and how alcohol education is to be given is far from uniform across the country and varies sometimes even from community to community within a state."

For alcohol education to be effective, says DISCUS, "it must be scientifically correct and, above all, it must have practical value for young people. They need to know how drinking can impair driving, typing, or athletic skills, or how it might affect judgment or reason. These facts they can understand and accept. Then young people can appreciate why abstinence is advisable on occasions when these abilities are needed."

DISCUS and some other groups are strongly opposed to any education methods that attempt to say flatly that alcohol is bad and no one should drink, contending that such "scare tactics" only alienate teenagers. (Of course, this attitude may be in these groups' own best interest.) "It is not necessary, or even appropriate, for a public school to adopt a position—either for or against drinking," says DISCUS. "Alcohol education should be neither pro alcohol nor abstinence-oriented. Schools must adopt an alternative—to teach responsibility in relation to alcohol."

Some educators believe that school officials can avoid the pitfall of offering students outdated, impractical instruction by integrating alcohol education with other related subjects, instead of treating it as a separate course. They point out that units on alcohol have often been inserted into courses on general science, biology, health education, physical education, driver and safety education, social studies, and home economics.

[91]

Adding to this, Donald G. Phelps, of the National Institute on Alcohol Abuse and Alcoholism (NIAAA), says: "Facts about alcohol should not be presented in isolation, but rather should be integrated into a school curriculum as a part of education for living."

NIAAA is especially encouraged by education programs that promote responsible decision making about the use of alcohol and encourage youth to develop healthy attitudes about themselves. Says Judith Katz, head of NIAAA's Youth Services branch, "The ultimate answer to a reduction in the devastating toll of alcoholism lies in the capacity of adults and youth to make sound decisions on the subject. Young people need clear, realistic information about alcohol use and misuse in order to make responsible decisions."

Most anti–drunk-driving groups agree that schools are a logical place to initiate alcohol prevention and education efforts, since they reach more young people than any other single institutional setting. But, they warn, before school-based alcohol-education programs can be effective, teachers and other adults who serve as "role models" must also be educated to deal with the issues surrounding alcohol use and misuse. Sums up Dr. Globetti: "How we teach may be more important than what we teach about alcohol, since drinking is a sensitive issue with adolescents."

One suggestion for reducing the number of teenage accidents on the highways is causing a maelstrom of controversy—that is the suggestion to eliminate high school driver-education programs in schools. Leon Robertson, of Yale University, who conducted a special study for the Insurance Institute for Highway Safety, says: "The increase in teenage [traffic] deaths in the 1960s and early 1970s resulted at least partly from a public policy specifically intended to reduce the crash involvement of teenaged drivers. The growth in publicly financed high school driver education greatly increased the number of sixteen- to seventeen-year-olds licensed, without reducing the number of crashes per licensed driver. The net result was more crashes."

Robertson based his comments on findings from a study in Connecticut where, in 1976, the state dropped funding for high school driver education. Consequently, eight municipalities and one regional school district eliminated the courses from their high school curricula.

Robertson's report indicated that elimination of the program in these communities over the next three years led to a 57 percent reduction in licensure among sixteen- to seventeen-year-olds, compared to a 9 percent decrease in communities that retained the program. Further, the communities without high school driver education experienced a 63 percent reduction in the crash rate among sixteen- and seventeen-year-olds on a population basis, compared with little change in the crash rate in communities that retained the programs.

According to the study: "About 75 percent of the sixteen- and seventeen-year-olds who could be expected to have been licensed if they had taken high school driver education waited until they were eighteen or older to be licensed when high school training was no longer available." The study also noted earlier research in England and the United States, which found that "more driver education was related to more licensed drivers," with the net result being higher crash involvement per capita for sixteen- and seventeen-year-olds.

Robertson concluded: "The intertwined and more far-reaching issue is whether or not sixteen- to seventeen-year-olds should be licensed to drive whatever their training. Many state laws do not allow persons less than eighteen years of age to vote, sign contracts, play pinball machines, and the like. And yet, persons apparently considered insufficiently mature for such activities are licensed to assume responsibility for operating vehicles that so commonly kill and maim."

Driver education professionals dispute the findings and conclusions of the Robertson and other studies. They contend that young drivers would be licensed and drive just as soon without the courses (although this was not true in the Connecticut case), and driving with fewer driving skills. Advocates of driver education says these programs provide young drivers with better starting skills than if they are taught to drive by their parents.

In recent years, some states have discussed increasing the minimum age of licensure to eighteen. Say Drs. Ronald S. Karpf and Allan F. Williams, in another report conducted for the Insurance Institute for Highway Safety: "This would undoubtedly be an effective policy, although not all of the more than 4,000 fatalities that result annually from the driving of sixteen- and seventeen-year-olds would be eliminated. Some might drive without licenses; those who would drive if allowed would become potential passengers; and to some extent, older drivers would substitute for sixteen- and seventeen-year-olds in providing transportation. Since sixteen- and seventeen-year-olds have very high crash rates per licensed driver, with or without mileage driven taken into account, the net result should be fewer fatalities when older drivers . . . substitute for them. It should be noted, however, that fatalities would be unlikely to be reduced in those cases in which eighteen- to twenty-year-old drivers, whose crash rates are as high or higher than those of sixteen- and seventeen-year-olds, replace them in providing transportation."

Dr. Karpf, Dr. Williams, and others acknowledge that not allowing licensure until age eighteen would likely create a furor, especially among teenagers, whose mobility would be restricted by such action. In their report, they say: "Although it can be argued that much of the driving at ages sixteen and seventeen is associated with recreational purposes and is therefore 'not essential,' this policy would result in inconveniences for many teenagers and their parents and others, and, in some cases, hardships."

But they add that these "negative effects" must be weighed against the substantial decrease in motor vehicle related deaths that would result. "One possible resolution to this debate would be to allow 'essential' driving by sixteen- and seventeen-year-olds, such as to and from places of employment."

Drs. Karpf and Williams also suggest the possibility of restricting the hours when teenagers may drive. They say, "Several states currently have regulations that prohibit some teenagers from driving during some late evening/early morning hours. So-called night curfews, if enforced, might substantially reduce fatalities involving teenage driving, since much of their driving is done at night. Almost half the fatal crashes of drivers less than eighteen years old take place from 8:01 p.m. to 4:00 a.m."

Indeed, in a study conducted by the Insurance Institute for Highway Safety, it was found that curfew laws in four states that limit night driving by sixteen-year-olds reduced teenagers' involvement in vehicle crashes by as much as 69 percent. The study compared accidents in Pennsylvania, New York, Maryland, and Louisiana, which have curfew laws, with comparable data in states that have no such laws. The conclusion was that during curfew hours, there were reductions of 60 percent in Pennsylvania, 62 percent in New York, 40 percent in Maryland, and 25 percent in Louisiana. The issues of high school driver education programs, and whether there should be a raising of the licensure age to eighteen, are likely to be hotly debated for some time to come, without any resolutions in sight.

Aside from classroom education, some anti–drunk-driving groups and organizations are conducting massive national public education programs targeted at reaching teenagers through such popular mediums as television, radio, newspapers, and magazines. One is the Distilled Spirits Council of the United States, and one of its most successful campaigns is called "Know Your Limits."

"Years ago, like everyone else, we said, 'If you drink, don't drive,' " says a DISCUS spokesperson. "But we learned that this approach was a wasted effort. No one paid any attention, and scare tactics were proven to be equally futile. For this reason, after studying surveys that demonstrated a clear relationship between number of drinks and the risk of an accident, we fostered a new and definitely more effective approach, the 'Know Your Limits' campaign." This involved, over the past few years, the distribution of more than 10 million wallet-size cards that show how the number of drinks a person has, individual body weight, and the time factor all relate to driving risks. This effort has been endorsed by the U.S. Department of Transportation.

Another ongoing project of DISCUS, in association with the National Football League and the Education Commission of the States, is focused on young people and features television commercials showing professional football stars urging teenagers to send for a free booklet. The literature discusses the pros and cons of drinking, emphasizing the fact that alcohol and driving do not mix. This project, endorsed by the National Parent-Teachers Association, has resulted in the distribution of millions of booklets and posters to tens of thousands of schools. It is estimated that some of the TV commercials alone reached audiences of up to 40 to 60 million people at a time.

DISCUS, the United States Brewers Association, and other organizations have also, for years, sponsored ads in popular national publications with circulations of tens of millions. These ads are aimed at highlighting the hazards of drinking and driving. One such ad, for example, has the headline, "Anyone Who Can't Walk a Straight Line Can't Drive One." The copy reads: "It's amazing how some people who can't even control their feet think they'll be able to control their car once they get behind the wheel. They're dead wrong."

"We recognize that our programs alone, no matter how well motivated or what message is conveyed, will not cause problems of drinking and driving to vanish overnight," says Sam D. Chilcote, Jr., a former president of DISCUS. "However, we believe such programs can constructively serve the cause of education in preventing alcohol abuse. They are designed to fulfill this function in an affirmative way by encouraging responsible drinking by those who drink."

Another form of public education that is having a telling impact on the teenager drunk-driving problem is the use of the popular media by noncelebrity individuals and groups. Daily, anti–drunk-driving spokespersons are appearing on local, regional, and, frequently, national radio and television talk shows, news programs, and specials. These people, including many teenagers, are armed with facts, figures, and positive arguments. Great numbers of them are people who have lost friends, sons, daughters, or brothers or sisters in alcohol-related accidents.

Other crusaders in the cause have told their stories about drunk driving to national magazines, and to metropolitan and rural newspapers. Thousands of articles on the subject have been appearing over the last two to three years. Anti–drunk-driving groups and organizations urge both teenagers and adults to get involved in such efforts in their area.

"Interest in the drunk-driving problem is at an unparalleled high level throughout this country," says Dr. Corgill. "Community and statewide groups of individuals can largely be credited with raising public awareness of the proportions of the problem."

Another concept catching on nationally involves "report drunk driver" programs. The National Transportation Safety Board, for example, has urged governors in all states to adopt such campaigns. "Studies have shown that drunken drivers generally do not believe they will be caught and, in fact, usually are not," said a board spokesperson. The board studied citizen drunken-driver reporting programs in five states—Colorado, Maryland, Nebraska, Utah, and Washington—and concluded that public participation could help ease the "disgraceful and frightening" death toll from drunken driving by increasing arrests of intoxicated drivers.

Under the program, citizens are asked to provide police with the most recent location of the suspect, as well as the direction of travel and the color, make, and license plate number of the vehicle. After a police officer locates the vehicle, he or she must observe indications of drunken driving before the driver can be stopped.

In Nebraska, where the reporting program is known as REDDI—Report Every Drunk Driver Immediately—nearly 3,000 suspected drunken drivers were reported to police over a one-year period. More than half of these were intercepted by police and arrested. Other participating states have reported similar results.

What else can be done? Anti–drunk-driving organizations believe many who play specialized roles in dealing with drinking and driving can contribute more. It is suggested, for example, that police officers familiarize themselves better with the symptoms of drunk driving, with appropriate techniques for handling the drunk driver, and with court procedures directed toward curbing the incidence of drunk driving. More suspected violators should be stopped and more intoxicated drivers should be arrested, rather than being let off with warnings.

Judges, anti–drunk-driving groups contend, are in a better position than anyone else in the community to alter public attitudes toward drinking and driving. They can point up the seriousness of the offense, influence problem drinkers to participate in treatment programs, and help establish a new set of community attitudes that are far less tolerant of alcohol abuse than those now in existence.

"Judges, in particular, need to crack down harder on drunk drivers, especially repeat offenders," declares Candy Lightner of MADD. "They have been too lenient for too long, and when they only 'slap the wrist' of a drunk driver, it almost is like encouraging them to continue. We encourage our MADD members to sit in on courtroom action and let the judges know we aren't happy with them. They don't like it, but that's tough."

Anti–drunk-driving campaigners are also pushing hard to get the cooperation of bartenders and tavern owners across the country. They point out that those who serve drinks to the public, including in some cases teenagers, have a vested interest in cooperating, because under many of the tougher new state laws, bartenders and bar proprietors can be held responsible should their customers become involved in alcohol-related accidents after leaving their places of business.

In Virginia, for example, warning flyers have been sent to bars across the commonwealth. They state: "Legally, if you serve an intoxicated person more alcohol, you could be convicted of a misdemeanor. The criminal penalty for the actual server of the beverage is a possible $500 fine and up to twelve months in jail. Also, your business license to sell alcoholic beverages may be suspended.

"And aside from the legal questions, you're in the position to protect another person's life. Therefore, it's up to you to know your customer's limit and take action if needed. The person who has had too much to drink probably can't remember how many drinks he's had, much less make a rational decision about his own ability to drive. On the other hand, you've been tabulating the number of drinks and by judging his weight and the amount of time he's been drinking, you should be able to size up the situation.

"Further, you're in a strategic position for helping him decide not to drive. Try the soft approach first. If the person asks for another drink, maybe you could bring a cup of coffee instead. The hint might be enough. If not, become a bit firmer. If need be, state firmly, 'My manager will not allow me to serve you another drink.' Then, see that your customer rides home with a friend, or call him a cab. You'll be protecting yourself, your patron, and others on the road. It's far easier to step in now than to live with the consequences of letting a drunk driver loose on the road."

Another approach advocated by some to help curb drunk driving involves having new drivers complete an alcohol highway safety program prior to the granting of a learner's permit or a driver's license. In many states, such programs are currently conducted for persons arrested for driving while intoxicated, and these programs are considered valuable by the courts, recipients, and others.

Proponents of the plan argue that the need is to teach people *before* they are arrested or in an accident. The basic format is established; the need now is to link the program to the beginning of a driving career and make it a general requirement in the same manner the driving test is. Further, it is contended, refresher courses should be required at regular intervals.

The Alliance of American Insurers believes that road and written driver renewal tests should be required at least every three years. "Licensing reform is badly needed," the alliance says. "Most licensing standards are more relevant to the 1940 road conditions than to today. For the drinking driver, existing standards are a giant loophole." The alliance also believes that questions on alcohol abuse should be included on driver's license tests.

One plan aimed at controlling drunk driving involves technical modifications of the vehicle. Ignition systems,

*Some automakers are experimenting with devices
in cars that "test" a driver's sobriety. In this
particular device, drivers must first punch in a code,
then repeat a combination of numbers flashed briefly
on the display. If they fail the test, the car will
not start, and they must wait a while before they
can take the test again.*

for example, could be modified to include coordination tests prior to unlocking. Such systems are already in existence in test automobiles and, like seat belts, could be required on all new cars. These systems could also have emergency overrides to allow the car to start through a bypass system, but would light an exterior signal to indicate the driver had started the car without the safety system.

One prototype system is being tested in California. If a driver who has had too much to drink fails to line up a series of arrows, he or she has to wait ten minutes before trying again. If the person overrides the device and drives without passing the "test," the car's lights flash and the horn blares if he or she drives over 10 miles (16 km) per hour, making the driver a conspicuous "target" for law-enforcement officers.

12 What You Can Do

What can you, as a young person, do to help solve the national teenage drunk-driving problem? Many authorities view the family as potentially the most effective agent in influencing drinking and driving decisions of youth, but it is often the most difficult resource to enlist.

Many parents go out of their way to avoid discussing such sensitive topics as sex, drugs, and drinking with their offspring. They may suspect that their children are involved in these activities, but they'd rather not ask and remove all doubt. Perhaps they think that if they ignore the situation long enough it will go away of its own accord. They fear unpleasant confrontations with their teenagers.

Sometimes parents don't remember what the teenage years are like. They don't remember that this is a time of experimentation and trying out adult behavior, or that both drinking and driving are expressions of independence. Parents may also be unaware of the heavy peer pressure on their teenage children to drink.

Many teenagers resent what they view as a double standard set by their parents. That is, their parents preach to them that it's bad to drink and drive, yet they themselves do it. They set a poor example for their own teenagers.

A nationwide survey of teenagers, conducted by the National Highway Traffic Safety Administration, showed that most teenagers still do respect their parents' views about driving and drinking. They want and expect their parents to talk with them about the subject, but they want it to be an open, two-way discussion, not a sermon that amounts to "We can, you can't, and that's all there is to it."

But teenagers should realize that it is frequently difficult for parents to engage in such frank and honest talks about sensitive subjects. Parents are apt to have a natural conflict between the desire to control their child's behavior to protect him or her from harm, and the recognition that some of these controls must be relaxed as their children move into their teens.

Despite all these problems, however, authorities believe that one of the best places to help solve the teenage drunk-driving problem is in the home. Parents and teenagers must strive to communicate more openly with each other. Here are some suggestions that experts say may prove helpful in conducting parent-teenage conversations on driving and drinking:

■ Bring up the subject only when all family members are in a calm frame of mind. The topic is explosive enough without adding emotional fuels to the fire.

■ Neither parents nor teenagers should make accusations or hand down ultimatums. Each side should hear the other out. For example, parents should realize that most teenagers are going to drink at some point in their lives, are going to drive, and are going to be passengers in cars driven by other teenagers. To forbid any activity with threats is unlikely to work. But parents should express their concern about mixing drinking and driving, and they should explain the dangers of this. Both parents and teenagers should learn all about alcohol and drugs and their effects on the body's systems.

■ Be patient. Don't expect to solve everything in one discussion. A good understanding of everything might take some time. The important thing is to let each other know that you are willing to talk about the issues, and to listen, too.

The National Highway Traffic Safety Administration and many other groups and organizations suggest that one key way for parents and teenagers to cope with the drunk-driving problem is to come to an agreement after having shared information, attitudes, and ideas. The agreement would cover specific ways that you and your family could help avoid a drinking-related accident. A sample agreement might deal with the following questions:

■ To avoid being driven home by a drunk friend, can a teenager get his or her parents' permission to drive the friend's car home?

■ If a teenager has driven to a party and subsequently had too much to drink, can he or she call home at any hour for a ride, no questions asked and no arguments? And if not, can he or she spend the night at the party-giver's house, as long as the parents are notified?

■ If a teenager with a car has had too much to drink or was driven by a friend who has had too much to drink, will the parents pay for a taxi to bring the teen home if the parents are not available to pick him or her up?

Sometimes it is easier, believe it or not, for parents and teenagers to agree than it is for teenagers and their friends to. Suppose, for example, you go to a keg party with a friend who is driving, and the friend has too much to drink. Chances are, when it's time to leave, your friend will believe that he or she can drive with no problem, and your natural feeling may be that it's easier to stay quiet than to make trouble about the ride. But authorities say this is the worst thing you can do, both for yourself and your friend.

They recommend that you politely offer to drive the car yourself, assuming *you* haven't had too much to drink. If this doesn't work, suggest that you both wait until your friend has had time to sober up. If you have to, and if you can get to them, take the car keys. If none of these strategies work, and your friend is still determined to drive, don't go with him or her. Riding with a drunk driver isn't cool, daring, or loyal—it's just plain dangerous. If you can, catch a ride home with someone else at the party. If you can't do that, call a friend or someone in your family and ask that person to come get you. It may be inconvenient at the time, but whoever you call—especially if it's your parents—would much rather come get you than see you go with your drunk friend.

One of the best ways to head off a confrontation, particularly in a group that is partying, is to agree among yourselves beforehand that one of you will be the "assigned" driver for the evening. Whoever that person is will pledge to stay sober.

Okay, suppose you are the driver. Everyone at the party is having a great time, and they're all calling you a party pooper because you are not drinking. The peer pressure is intense. What do you do?

Experts say that it is harder to turn down a drink than to accept one. But if you don't want to drink, don't. Usually, the best way to refuse a drink is with a simple, direct "No, thanks." You don't need to make apologies, excuses, or arguments. If you feel comfortable about not drinking, others will probably just accept it and not hassle you.

But what if you are driving and you do drink too much? The same advice applies to you as it would to a friend. Have someone else drive the car. If no one else is available, call a friend or a relative. Call your mom or dad and simply explain the situation.

If you are the one hosting the party, authorities say you should have food available to your guests. This slows the reaction of alcohol in the system. Don't force drinks on guests, and if someone obviously is drinking too much, slow that person down. He or she may be angry at you at the moment but will later realize you have done him or her a big favor. Also, stop serving alcohol an hour before the party is to end. This will give guests who have had too much to drink time to sober up.

If someone is driving and has had too much to drink at your party, arrange for someone else to get that person home, or even put the drinker up for the night. This, too, may be inconvenient, but how would you feel if a friend had an accident on the way home after getting boozed up at your place?

Some of these measures may seem a bit extreme. They are, and for a very good reason. Think about it. When a friend of yours has too much to drink and gets behind the wheel of a car, he or she is a threat not only to himself or herself but to everyone on the road.

Says the National Highway Traffic Safety Administration: "Sometimes it takes courage to be a good friend, but it's worth it. And you can always count on the gratitude of your friend when he or she has had a chance to sober up and think more clearly."

13
Lasting Scars

In a split second, young lives can be ruined by the grinding crash of thousands of pounds of metal. The lasting scars—to those who survive—can often be more than physical. Even if you escape serious injury during an accident you have caused by driving while drinking, you risk the danger of having a criminal record for the rest of your life or being imprisoned.

But perhaps worst of all is the overwhelming emotional trauma of knowing you have maimed or killed someone else, either a friend, a stranger, or both, because of your irresponsible act of driving while drinking. This is something you will have to live with for the rest of your life. Is it worth it?

Consider the case of "Paul," a seventeen-year-old boy who, coming home from a beer party, rammed his parents' new car into a parked truck. Paul walked away from the wreckage with only scratches, but his best friend, another seventeen-year-old who was a passenger in the car, was killed instantly. Paul's blood-alcohol level at the time was in excess of .10, yet he "got off" with a license suspension, a fine of $150, and a suspended jail sentence in lieu of his participation in an alcohol-safety program.

But did he get off easy? Listen to what he has to say about the experience: "I guess I have relived that night a thousand times since it happened. And each time is more terrifying than the last. All I can see in my mind is the bloodied body of my friend, lying there, still and silent.

"He had begged me to slow down, but I was too cocky. I thought I was in control. I thought it was great sport to see how fast I could go—to scare him. It all happened so fast.

"I still have nightmares about it. I remember the only sound I could hear after the crash was the hissing of the radiator. It was eerie. I tried to revive my friend, but there was no movement, nothing. At first I couldn't believe what had occurred. I couldn't accept it. Maybe the alcohol had made me sort of crazy. It took a long time for reality to set in.

"But when it did, it was terrible. When I sobered up and fully realized what I had done, the shock and grief were almost unbearable. I wanted to die. I've wished over and over that I had been the one killed, not my friend. And then there was a deep, helpless feeling that there was nothing I could do about it. I felt shame and guilt.

"I couldn't face his parents. I couldn't face my parents. What could I say? A wrecked car can be fixed, or a new car can be bought. But you can't bring someone back to life. And I knew just saying I was sorry really meant nothing. It was really an awful feeling.

"When I went back to school, I could see the expressions in the students' faces. I knew what they were thinking. It was very awkward and humiliating. Even the few who tried to sympathize with me, saying it could have happened to anyone, didn't help. Because it didn't happen to anyone. It happened to me.

"I'd give everything I have, or ever will have, to be able to erase that night, but I realize that can't be. I guess time will help, but I know that one instant, that one flash of a second, will last my lifetime.

"Do I have any advice for others? Yes, and it's very simple. Don't drink and drive. The odds may be a thousand-to-one of anything happening to you, like it did to me. But even if they are, believe me, it's not worth the risk."

Bibliography

SPECIAL PUBLICATIONS

"Communications Strategies on
    Alcohol and Highway Safety"
"How to Talk to Your Teenager about
    Drinking and Driving"
"An Activist's Guide for Curbing the Drunk Driver"
"Young People and Alcohol"

U.S. Department of Transportation, National Highway
Traffic Safety Administration, Washington, D.C.
20590.

"Facts about Alcohol and Alcoholism"
"Talking to Your Teenager about
    Drinking and Driving"
"Guide to Alcohol Programs for Youth"
"Drugs and Driving"

U.S. Department of Health and Human Services, Public
Health Service, Alcohol, Drug Abuse and Mental
Health Administration, National Institute on Alcohol
Abuse and Alcoholism, 5600 Fishers Lane, Rockville,
Maryland 20857.

"No One Answer: A Closer Look at Teenage Drinking"
"If You Choose to Drink, Drink Responsibly"
"Straight Talk about Alcohol—
    for Parents and Teenagers"
"DISCUS Programs to Combat
    Alcohol Abuse Problems"

Distilled Spirits Council of the United States, Inc., 425
13th St., N.W., Suite 1300, Washington, D.C. 20004.

"Facts About Teen Alcohol/Drug Use and Driving"
"Danger Ahead: Marijuana on the Road"

The National Association of Independent Insurers, 2600
River Road, Des Plaines, Illinois 60018.

"Summary of State Laws Relating to Drunk Driving"
American Insurance Association, 1025 Connecticut
Ave., N.W., Washington, D.C. 20036.

"Deaths of Teenagers as Passengers in Motor Vehicles"
    Preliminary Report, September 1981

"Teenage Drivers and Motor Vehicle Deaths"
    Preliminary Report, September 1981

"Status Report: Drinking-Driving Laws—What Works?"
    April 16, 1981

"Status Report: Teens and Autos—
    A Deadly Combination," September 23, 1981

Insurance Institute for Highway Safety, 600 Watergate,
Washington, D.C. 20037.

"Remarks of the President on Creation of Drunk Driving
    Commission," April 14, 1982, the White House,
    Washington, D.C.

"Driver Safety," U.S. Senate Report, April 26, 1982,
    Calendar No. 512, Report No. 97-360.

"Teenage Drinking," Editorial Research Reports, Vol. 1, No. 18, May 15, 1981. Published by Congressional Quarterly Inc., 1414 22nd St., N.W., Washington, D.C. 20037.

"Drug Abuse: A Realistic Primer for Parents," Do It Now Foundation, National Media Center, P.O. Box 5115, Phoenix, Arizona 85010.

"Don't Let Your Loved One Be a Victim," Mothers Against Drunk Driving, 5330 Primrose, Suite 146, Fair Oaks, California 95628.

"Guide to More Effective Drunk Driving Legislation in the States," Highway Users Federation, June 1982.

MAGAZINE ARTICLES

"Can Students Be Taught to Mix Alcohol and Gasoline—Safely?" *Journal of School Health,* November 1971

"Alcohol and Other Drugs Related to Young Drivers' Traffic Accident Involvement," *Journal of Safety Research,* June 1976

"Teenage Drinking and Driving," *California Highway Patrolman,* May 1978

"Teens, Drugs and Alcohol—On the Road Again," *Journal of American Insurance,* fall-winter 1978

"Minimum Drinking Age Laws and Teenage Drinking," *Psychiatric Opinion,* March 1979

"Marijuana and Driving: The Sobering Truth," *Reader's Digest,* May 1979

"Many States Reconsidering Lowered Drinking-Age Laws," *Traffic Safety,* July 1979

"Puff, the Dangerous Driver," *Car and Driver,* June 1980

"Raising the Legal Drinking Age Is a Sobering Experience," *Journal of American Insurance,* spring 1981

"Patterns of Teenaged Driver Involvement in Fatal Motor Vehicle Crashes: Implications for Policy Choice," *Journal of Health Politics, Policy and Law,* summer 1981

"How to Get Alcohol off the Highway," *Family Circle,* July 1, 1981

"How Fast Can You Die in a Speeding Car?" *Transport Times,* July 1981

"They're MADD as Hell," *Time,* August 3, 1981

"The Effect of Raising the Legal Minimum Drinking Age on Fatal Crash Involvement," *Journal of Legal Studies,* September 1981

"Death on the 'High'-Way," *Saturday Evening Post,* September 1981

"Alcohol, Pot . . . and Sudden Death," *Saturday Evening Post,* October 1981

"Drink Young, Die Young," *Minnesota Sheriff,* autumn 1981

"Curbing Drunk Drivers," *Newsweek,* January 25, 1982

"Death on the 'High'-Ways: Driving on Drink & Pot," *Family Magazine,* January 1982

"Drunk Driving: A License to Kill," *Reader's Digest,* February 1982

"The War against Drunk Drivers," *Newsweek,* September 13, 1982

"Glad to Be SADD," *Listen Magazine,* October 1982

Sources for Additional Information

Alcohol Education for Youth, Inc.
1500 Western Ave.,
Albany, New York 12203

American Automobile Association
1025 Gatehouse Road,
Falls Church, Virginia 22041

American Insurance Association
1025 Connecticut Ave., N.W.,
Washington, D.C. 20036

Do It Now Foundation
National Media Center, P.O. Box 5115,
Phoenix, Arizona 85010

Distilled Spirits Council of the United States, Inc.
425 13th St., N.W., Suite 1300,
Washington, D.C. 20004

Insurance Institute for Highway Safety
600 Watergate,
Washington, D.C. 20037

Mothers Against Drunk Driving
5330 Primrose, Suite 146,
Fair Oaks, California 95628

National Association of Governors'
  Highway Safety Representatives
444 N. Capitol Street, Suite 524,
Washington, D.C. 20001

National Association of Independent Insurers
2600 River Road,
Des Plaines, Illinois 60018

National Beer Wholesalers Association
  of America, Inc.
5205 Leesburg Pike,
Falls Church, Virginia 22041

National Council on Alcoholism, Inc.
733 Third Ave.,
New York, N.Y. 10017

National Safety Council
425 N. Michigan Ave.,
Chicago, Illinois 60611

United States Brewers Association, Inc.
1750 K. Street, N.W.,
Washington, D.C. 20006

U.S. Department of Health and Human Services, Alcohol, Drug Abuse and Mental Health Administration,
  National Institute on Alcohol Abuse and Alcoholism
5600 Fishers Lane, Rockville, Maryland 20857

U.S. Department of Transportation,
National Highway Traffic Safety Administration,
Washington, D.C. 20590

Index